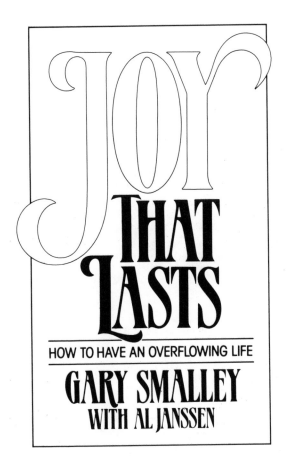

Joy

THAT LASTS

HOW TO HAVE AN OVERFLOWING LIFE

GARY SMALLEY
WITH AL JANSSEN

PYRANEE
BOOKS

Zondervan Publishing House
Grand Rapids, Michigan

Pyranee Books are published by
Zondervan Publishing House
1415 Lake Drive, S.E.
Grand Rapids, Michigan 49506

JOY THAT LASTS

Library of Congress Cataloging in Publication Data

Smalley, Gary.
  Joy that lasts.

  1. Christian life—1960–   . I. Janssen, Al. II. Title.
BV4501.2.S484   1986   248.4   86-22622
ISBN 0-310-46290-8

Edited by Julie Ackerman Link

Unless otherwise indicated, Scripture references are from the
New American Standard Bible, © 1960, 1962, 1963, 1968, 1971,
1972 by The Lockman Foundation.

Printed in the United States of America

86 87 88 89 90 / 10 9 8 7 6 5 4 3 2 1

To four outstanding, supportive couples,
who know the secret of having JOY THAT LASTS:
Jim and Jan Stewart, Ben and Ann Kitchings,
Charles and Dorothy Shellenberger,
and Rick and Joan Malouf

To protect the identity of those I have counseled, I have changed the names and circumstances in many stories. Likewise, certain details of my personal life have been altered, especially in chapter one, to protect the privacy of several individuals. In all cases, however, I have attempted to convey the essence of the experience and communicate as accurately as possible the underlying principles at work.

Contents

1

Reaching Bottom Is the First Step Up

EVERY CRISIS, no matter the magnitude, is a step toward an enriched life, but try to explain that concept to a hurting couple.

Gerald, a tanned, athletic-looking man dressed in a golf shirt and custom slacks, wept in my office. Next to him, with a dazed look on her face, sat his wife, Martha. Although flooded by the sunlight that brightens Phoenix more than three hundred days a year, this couple could not escape their gloom as they told me about their teenage son, Don, who had rejected all of their standards.

This couple had done their best to raise Don in a Christian environment, but now that he was an adolescent he spent most of his time at parties, often strung out on drugs, with no apparent ambition for school or a career. This personal tragedy had robbed Gerald of his enthusiasm for his job as president of his own company. The possessions he'd worked so long and so hard to acquire—two homes, expensive cars, a forty-foot yacht—no longer satisfied him.

Martha's hurt ran even deeper. For years women at the club and at social events had spoken of her family as a model. Now she overheard snatches of conversation from those same women using her family tragedy as the latest bit of gossip. Each new painful episode that unfolded with her son added to her shame and left her emotionally exhausted. Martha felt she had little reason to continue living.

Stories like this permeate society, and they are not limited to the wealthy. No matter what our circumstances, whether we own much or little, we cannot live for long without feeling cheated by life. We eventually will experience despair and discouragement.

All of us will one day lose loved ones through death or separation. Illness will hamper some of our lives. Some of us will lose precious possessions, be victimized by violent crimes, jilted by friends, financially ruined by bad investments, heartbroken by rebellious children, or unjustly fired from well-paying jobs. And some of us will waste our time worrying that these things will happen. Every day people face rejection, loneliness, and hurt feelings. And they envy the success and apparent happiness of others.

Many believe God is pulling a cruel prank when He allows us or loved ones to suffer unjustly. Others repeat (or whisper under their breath) words similar to those spoken by the people in Isaiah's time: "My way is hidden from the Lord, and the justice due me escapes the notice of my God" (Isaiah 40:27). Those of us who have felt betrayed by God understand Gerald and Martha's discouragement.

Gerald and Martha did not know, however, that *their troubles actually brought them a step closer to the richest life possible.* They were on the brink of a life filled with joy and peace without realizing how close they were.

How could I help them? They would not accept simplistic formulas. They hurt, and they needed to know that someone understood their pain. They didn't need theoretical answers; they needed hope. A road map and a few words of encouragement from me wouldn't be enough to help them find their own way out of their circumstances. They needed a personal guide.

"He jests at scars, that never felt a wound," Romeo said in Shakespeare's *Romeo and Juliet.* The only way for me to help Gerald and Martha was to "feel their wound." Although I had never experienced the pain of having a rebellious child, I too had known rejection. Nine years earlier I had been deeply wounded by my closest friend. Although the crisis didn't involve my family, I felt the pain of rejection as intensely as any parent of a wayward child. Yet that difficult experience opened for me the door to the most enriching discovery of my life.

To help Gerald and Martha I told them my personal story of rejection and discovery. I had helped my best friend build a small company into a leader in the industry, only to lose my position and friendship. Then for two years I wallowed in a marsh of despair, wondering if I could ever again experience the level of fulfillment I'd found in my work and unique relationship. In the midst of my mental and emotional anguish, however, I had discovered the doorway that leads to fulfillment. Quietly I told Gerald and Martha my story.

As a young man fresh out of graduate school, I had met Dale at the church where I was assistant pastor. He owned a small company that sold health food products. Through seminars and written materials, he taught people how to live healthy and fulfilling lives.

Dale's charisma captivated me. Like a modern-day John the Baptist, he called people to a combination of well-rounded physical health and moral purity. And he lived what he preached. He was totally committed to his work and spoke boldly about selling people a great product while bringing America back to Christian values. Accepting his invitation to work for him was the easiest decision I'd ever made.

My wife, Norma, didn't share my enthusiasm. In spite of my excitement, she told me several times that she felt I would regret working for him. But I "knew" better. I believed Dale was a modern-day prophet who had a vision to change America, and I was going to help him.

That was in 1968. Six of us manned the company headquarters in a suburb of Denver. We doubled the size of the business in the first year and doubled it again the next. We could hardly contain our enthusiasm when we realized that everyone in the United States would be using our products within fifteen years if we continued the same rate of expansion.

I began to arrange for major hotel ballrooms to hold Dale's meetings. We packed out conferences in Seattle, Long Beach, Chicago, Dallas, and Kansas City. To see entire hotels and convention centers filled as Dale motivated people to live healthy lives staggered me. And then to see people fill our coffers by buying our line of natural food products, books, and other materials was more than I could believe.

I opened regional offices in ten cities, hired managers to supervise warehouses filled with our products, and trained a growing number of distributors to promote Dale's philosophy. On the road every month, I interviewed prospective employees, approved office leases, negotiated agreements with hotels and convention centers, and conducted motivational seminars of my own for our employees.

My most significant memories, however, were not of packed conferences, exciting business transactions, or constant travel and first-class accommodations. What meant the most were the times Dale and I slipped away to a remote cabin in the Colorado Rockies. There we would spend a couple of days praying, developing new conference and promotional materials, dreaming of new products for our research department, and plotting strategy to take our message and products beyond the U.S. border to the entire world.

Every few hours we would take a break and toss rocks into a trash can, competing like two kids to see who could make the most shots. Sometimes in the evening Dale would tire, and I'd keep him awake, motivated by the thought of sending new material to our distributors or conducting our seminar in a new city. People's lives were being transformed by Dale's work, and I passionately believed it had to spread as quickly as possible.

Dale was everything I could want in a friend; in fact, in many ways he was like a brother. We shared much more than the vision to help people. Since we were nearly the same size, we often borrowed each other's clothes. Many times I walked into my office and found a new shirt or tie on my desk—a present from my best of friends.

Sometimes Dale would call me late at night, embarrassed that he couldn't remember who had borrowed his car. I would drive the four blocks to our headquarters to pick him up and often we'd go out for a late dinner. Inevitably I would have to pay because money meant little to Dale. Frequently he didn't even have his wallet. But he was a generous man. When Norma's car was in the shop, I'd simply go into Dale's office and he'd give me the keys to his car. His door was always open, and I was involved in most of his meetings.

Dale was married, but spent little time with his wife. The many exciting things happening at work demanded most of his time and energy, and our friendship took a great deal of his time as well. In many ways, I too made my relationship with Dale a higher priority than my own wife and family. I believed I was in an ideal situation that would last until I retired. Dale and I shared our possessions, our personal dreams, and our vision for the company.

In the ninth year of our intimate friendship I

began to detect a subtle change. By then our head-quarters complex teemed with more than one hundred employees. We were no longer a small, intimate family. New managers with MBA degrees had strong ideas about how to run the company. Personality clashes and distrust replaced the warmth of our office. Upper management jockied for Dale's time.

One afternoon I walked into Dale's office and asked for his car keys. Without looking up from his paperwork, he informed me that we had a new policy. "The staff will no longer borrow each other's cars," he said, and with that I was dismissed. In the days that followed I was also informed that I had to knock before entering Dale's office and that I was no longer needed in some important meetings I would have attended a few months earlier.

Like a jealous suitor, I was hurt and confused by this sudden change in our working and personal relationship. I kept wondering what I had said or done to cause Dale's response.

In the week that followed I learned, "through the grapevine," that some of the new management team did not approve of my qualifications and were threatened by the amount of access and influence I had with Dale. So almost overnight they had gotten me moved from the fireplace off into a cold, damp corner.

During this same time of tension and change, our accountant, a longtime friend, came to me with devastating news. He felt sure that three of the company officers who were very close to Dale were engaging in unethical business practices with company funds.

Dale had established such high standards with his product, conferences, and company that we enjoyed an unblemished reputation with our customers and suppliers. The behavior of these men would eat away at our credibility and threaten the existence of our company.

I made an appointment for the accountant and me to see Dale. On a Friday afternoon we laid before him all the facts about our staff problem. Then I made what I believed was a very logical recommendation: that we fire the three managers and deal openly with the people that were affected, before any serious damage was done to the company.

Dale rejected my idea. Looking me straight in the eye he said that he appreciated my information but he didn't believe the offenses merited any disciplinary action.

This was not the Dale I knew. I felt as if I were a stranger in the presence of a man I once knew intimately. As I sensed how far apart we had moved I felt the lifeblood of our relationship draining away.

Throughout the next week I was so emotionally devastated that I could barely muster enough strength to return to work. For nine years all my energy had been devoted to Dale and his cause. But suddenly the cause was hollow, and so was I. Rejected by my best friend and completely drained of my enthusiasm, I didn't know where to turn.

Years later, Dale admitted that keeping those managers was a mistake. Company growth leveled off and even declined as a result of that decision. For me, however, the effect was immediately devastating. For several days severe depression sapped all my energy, and I lost all enthusiasm for the cause that had captivated my life for so many years.

Gerald and Martha listened attentively as I related my story. When I stopped for a moment, Martha asked, "How did you ever overcome that?"

I told her that for a long time there was no one I could talk to. Dale had been my spiritual confidant. He was respected in the Christian community, so I didn't feel I could seek counsel from anyone who knew about our work without sounding like a disgruntled employee. It was even difficult to express my fears to Norma. She had warned me about working with Dale, and I wouldn't humble myself to admit her intuition had been right.

It took nearly two years and a career change before I understood the answer. In the process, I began to realize a tremendous truth:

Trials can be our greatest experience, for they can lead to the source of lasting joy.

Through this devastating experience I discovered the secret to a life so fulfilling that today it is almost impossible for circumstances to rob me of my joy for any length of time.

I drew a picture of a cup and explained that it represented my life. Then I showed Gerald and Martha how I had filled my cup from the wrong sources. Dale and my job had satisfied me for almost nine years, but when things started going wrong they became like acid, eating holes in the walls of my life until everything fulfilling and meaningful had drained out. Through that experience I learned the secret to keeping my cup filled. There was one source that would not only fill it, but cause it to overflow!

I shared with Gerald and Martha the same principles that are the basis for this book, and when they left my office, they looked hopeful. A few weeks later Gerald called to tell me that he and his wife had gained a new purpose in life. Even their son recognized the change. Gerald kept in touch over the next two years and told me how he and Martha were experiencing fulfillment and peace on a daily basis, regardless of their circumstances. Gradually their son began to change his lifestyle and eventually he entered a local community college to prepare for a career in business.

Many of us are facing difficult circumstances. Some of us hurt because we've been rejected by someone we love. Some of us have climbed over fences to find greener pasture but found only desert instead. Some of us have followed a rainbow only to find the pot of gold an illusion. And some of us are worried that the good life we enjoy may evaporate.

As incredible as it may seem, those who recognize themselves in any of the above circumstances are on the brink of discovering an exciting life. In fact, problems are the tools that help us fill our lives with lasting joy, peace, and love. But most of us do not even recognize the tools, much less know how to use them.

I never understood this myself until I lost almost everything of value. During my search for meaning and purpose after my devastating experience with Dale I discovered several biblical tools that turned my tragedy into triumph. In the following pages I'd like to help you identify and learn to use them in your own life. These tools help us build up our self-worth, regulate our negative emotions such as anger, worry, fear, and envy for our benefit, and equip us to go on a treasure hunt to find the "gold" that is buried in every trial.

The message that God intends us to live in a perpetual oasis may encourage us for a season, but before long we will run into trials, and with them a dry, barren desert. Crossing a desert unprepared can be deadly. My prayer is that this book will help you prepare for inevitable desert experiences and show you how to find the true source of refreshment. This discovery will lead you to the source that is always running over, never running dry. I missed out on this refreshment for years because I kept trying to find something tangible that would finally satisfy me. I learned instead that even having it all wasn't enough.

2

Having It All Isn't Enough

STEVE AND BRENDA were excited about their future. They were young, talented professionals who deeply loved each other. Steve had just completed medical school and looked forward to a surgical career. Brenda was a nurse at the county hospital. They had dated since high school, and now that Steve had finished his training they finally felt free to marry. Their wedding was the talk of their small town. They had so much going for them—a promising financial future, important positions in the community, and a deep love and commitment to each other. They never could have imagined the tragedy that would shatter their expectations and destroy their lives.

Four weeks after their wedding, Brenda contracted a rare form of hepatitis from an emergency room patient she had treated. Doctors immediately hospitalized her but their treatment was ineffective. She weakened daily and within a week had died.

Steve's dreams died with her. He had never

considered the possibility that the one he loved could be taken from him so abruptly. After the funeral, overwhelmed by his devastating loss, he walked aimlessly around town for hours. In the following days he couldn't bear to go to his office. Often he would sit in his darkened apartment, tears streaming down his face.

Two weeks after the funeral, in an act of desperation, Steve tried to take his own life with an overdose of pills. If his parents had not become concerned when he didn't answer their phone calls, Steve's attempt would have succeeded. Now, several years later, Steve still struggles with chronic depression and has never reached his potential as a surgeon. His life is frozen in a tragic experience from his past.

Most of us will never face such a tragedy, but sooner or later all of us must come to grips with life's insecurity. We may move through life unaffected for weeks, months, even years, but eventually each of us will suffer some form of loss or disillusionment. The feeling of loss will be more traumatic for some than for others, but all of us will have to deal with its effects.

I never considered suicide after my experience with Dale, but like Steve, I experienced a deep sense of loss. For several months after leaving the company, I frequently woke up at three or four o'clock in the morning with my stomach churning like a stormy sea. I desperately wanted to understand why I was experiencing such misery. If the Christian life that I believed and spoke about was true, why was I so unhappy? Why couldn't I rise above this disappointment and move on with my life?

One morning I awoke at four o'clock with the familiar pangs of anxiety engulfing me. To keep from disturbing Norma, I quietly slipped out of bed and tiptoed down the hall. My eight-year-old son heard me. "What are you doing, Dad?" Greg whispered.

"I'm going downstairs to study," I told him.

"Can I go with you?"

After pouring Greg a cup of juice I sat down with him at the kitchen table and admitted to him that I was going through a struggle and couldn't seem to find the answer. He listened and tried to understand. "Greg, there has to be a reason why I keep getting my feelings so hurt. Do you remember the time we went fishing and you lost that big trout? You cried and I had to hold you for a long time?" Greg nodded. "That's a little like how I've felt for the past few weeks. I feel like I had a trophy fish right at the edge of the boat—but it got away. I feel such a deep sense of loss that I can't feel joy anymore."

Greg didn't understand, but talking to him helped me crystallize my thoughts. Perhaps if I could explain what I felt to an eight-year-old boy, I could understand it myself. "Greg, I think I've been making the same mistake over and over. Maybe that's why I'm so miserable." I looked at his nearly empty cup of juice and suddenly had an idea. "It's like my life is a cup, and until recently it was filled with joy and peace and love. But lately a big hole has been drilled in it and all the life has drained out. Instead of joy filling my cup, anger and fear and hurt feelings have taken its place."

"But what made that hole?" Greg asked.

As I talked, I realized I had been expecting relationships to keep my cup filled. I grabbed a note pad and drew a picture. "I think it's becoming clearer to me! Greg, tell me if this makes sense."

I drew as I talked. "As I think about it, Greg, I'm not looking for life just in relationships; actually I'm looking for life in at least four different places. And fulfillment from these four places floods into my life through a network of hoses and faucets. The problem is, someone has turned off the spigot!" I showed Greg the picture and he said he understood.

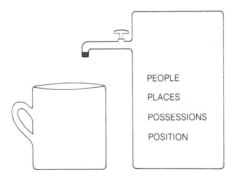

PEOPLE

PLACES

POSSESSIONS

POSITION

For the first time I began to realize my major mistake: I was expecting to find fulfillment in people, places, possessions, and position.

Not only did I no longer receive fulfillment from these sources, it was as if the satisfaction they once had given me was now destroying me.

That late-night conversation with Greg changed my life. For the first time I began to understand why my emotional and spiritual life had been like a small sailboat on a large lake. On nice days with gentle breezes I would skim across life's surface, refreshed by the wind and invigorated by the spray. But when the storm clouds came (and they always do), I had no safe harbor to sail to and no anchor strong enough to help me ride out the storm. The lake that once provided pleasure and fulfillment suddenly became life-threatening.

In my own personal life, and with people I am trying to help, like Gerald and Martha, I always take time to look closely at the four areas that cause so many of us to miss out on a satisfying life: people, places, possessions, position.

PEOPLE—WE CAN'T CONTROL THEM

For the first thirty-five years of my life I thought people were supposed to make me happy. My wife, children, friends, relatives, boss, fellow employees— all were part of a group I felt should fill my cup. This belief caused my problem with Dale. I enjoyed our friendship so much that I began to expect it to continue unchanged forever. In a subtle way, I shifted from following Dale's leadership to expecting him to cooperate with my goal of enjoying our unique friendship. I became more interested in our meetings than in the goals of the corporation. Preparing material and planning new strategies, at first a means to help more people, became ends in themselves— ways to spend time with Dale.

I had similar expectations of my family. I wanted them to appreciate the great movement I was in and to serve me by submitting their desires to the goals of this great work. I remember one winter day in particular when Dale called a special meeting at 5:00 in the afternoon. Through my office window I could see Norma waiting in the car for me. Snow had started to fall, and the children were pleading to play outside but weren't dressed appropriately. Rather than excuse myself from the meeting, even to tell her how much longer I'd be, I expected her to under- stand and wait patiently in the cold with the kids for forty-five minutes. After all, I was helping to bring a spiritual and physical revival to our country. What could possibly be more important?

It was years before I realized, with grief and embarrassment, that I'd selfishly expected my wife and kids to serve my ambition. No wonder Norma and I weren't receiving much joy in our lopsided relationship.

I see this attitude frequently in dating and marriage relationships. Take, for example, a woman who dreams for years about finding "Mr. Wonderful." She believes this man will fulfill her deepest longing for intimacy. She pictures him sitting next to her on an overstuffed love seat in front of a warm fire, his arm around her, talking for hours. She sees them discussing their plans for the future, their next vacation, and how they'll redecorate the living room. She knows he will diligently fix things around the house, keep her car running smoothly, and be there to support and encourage her when she is discouraged. She often thinks of her husband-to-be as a waterfall cascading into her life, a never-ending source of fulfillment that will make her life overflow with meaning.

This woman doesn't know she is setting herself up for the very heartache she is trying to escape. A few weeks into marriage she will realize that her husband, in many ways, can't or won't cooperate with her expectations. The relationship she expected to bring security may actually make her more *insecure.* Her husband may be the type who notices every attractive girl who walks by. He may be so wrapped up in his work that he shows little interest in her work or activities. He may be too tired to fix her car or make necessary household repairs. Even his interest in touching her may seem to have only sexual connotations.

Before long this woman, who once had so many dreams, begins to feel used and taken for granted, almost as if he had hired her as a maid. Not only is he not filling her cup, but his insensitivity has started to wear small holes in it and her emotional energy is draining out. Eventually she may even lose the level of love, happiness, and peace she had when she entered the marriage.

When her husband fails to meet her needs, she may think of an alternative: "If my husband isn't going to meet my needs," she reasons, "I'll have a family. Children running around the house are what I need to be fulfilled!" Too late she will discover that children, rather than filling her cup, have an amazing capacity to drill very large holes in it.

A man may also enter marriage with many expectations. He pictures how his wife will respond to him. Each day she will comment on how gifted he is as a lover, husband, and father. Without question, she will prepare delicious meals every night and always respond warmly to his sexual desires.

But soon he too discovers that not only is she unable to fill his cup, but she chips off the enamel until leaky cracks develop. Like her, his insecurity increases, and he may begin to think he married the wrong person. He may even begin to look around for another woman who he thinks will better meet his needs and become his ultimate "cup filler."

Husbands and wives are not unique. Many others are frustrated because they look to people to fulfill their expectations. Children may long for greater love and better communication with their parents. Parents may feel "taken advantage of" by their children. Employees often feel that employers do not care about them as people. Employers may feel that employees have no sense of loyalty or gratitude. And many Christians feel betrayed when certain "super Christians" succumb to temptation and turn out to be just as human and just as prone to failure as anyone else.

In Proverbs we read, "Hope deferred makes the heart sick" (13:12). Many husbands, wives, children, employees, employers, and friends put their hope for fulfillment in other people, which eventually leaves them empty and frustrated inside. Researchers like Albert Bandura and other sociologists believe this is a major cause of many social problems. Their research on anger and acts of violence related to anger shows that a key contributing factor is "frustrated expectations," the same thing that leads to divorce, runaway youth, suicide, battered mates, kidnapping, drug and alcohol abuse.

I am grateful I finally began to see this principle, because my unrealistic expectations of others kept me from gaining the fulfillment I sought. People, no matter how perfect, could never fill my life.

But if that is true, where can we turn?

PLACES—WE GET BORED WITH THEM

John and his wife, Joan, went through emotions similar to mine. Each expected fulfillment from the other. When they didn't find it they thought a new home might help. They built a beautiful house on several acres in a suburb of San Francisco, but they still had trouble getting along. John felt they needed a change of location, so he built a beautiful mountain cabin. That didn't solve the problem either, however, because they fought just as well in their cabin as in their spacious San Francisco home.

Relying on a location or special place to bring us lasting joy is like taking a snapshot of a beautiful setting. When we get the picture developed it never quite recaptures the beauty we beheld.

Joan wasn't impressed by the places John

provided for her, so she decided to test her wings, to get free from the man who was robbing her of joy. When she left she took their child with her.

After several months of being on her own away from home, Joan discovered the secret of having her cup filled with lasting joy. John noticed such a change in her that he asked what she had found. Her explanation led to the restoration of their relationship as he too realized that permanent happiness didn't dwell in a spectacular home or mountain cabin.

People today look to all types of places to fill their cups. In the United States, the first place most couples expect to find fulfillment is in their own home. Indeed, few of us can be content without a proper home. We're concerned about the neighborhood, the number of bathrooms, the view, and appropriate furnishings and coordinated interior decoration. Whether we rent or own or live in an apartment or a sprawling split-level, we expect pleasure and satisfaction from our home. We even feel cheated if we're not living in the right location. But getting our dream home can cause more anxiety than not getting it. Often we end up worried about making mortgage payments, how or where to add another room, and what security system to install to protect our investment.

When Norma and I finally bought our first house five years after we were married, everything about it—the smells, the fresh paint, the new neighbors—excited us. But after the initial thrill wore off, we noticed how loud the neighbor's dog barked and the continual loud music from their patio. They did nothing to control their dandelions, so their weeds quickly spread to our grass.

As we settled into the routine of living, our house became ordinary. Our friends' new home was more spacious and had more conveniences. We began to think we too needed those things. But the more things we bought, the more things needed fixing. The bigger the house, the bigger and more expensive the problems and the more time and effort they consumed.

I admit that I have enjoyed fleeting moments of satisfaction from our home in Arizona, but it frustrates me more than it satisfies me. My garage door breaks an average of twice a year. The hinges on the back gate have fallen off. Swarms of aphids have set up housekeeping on our rosess. Dust from the expansion of our family room kept circulating through the house after construction. My lawn is always dying, either because I gave it too much water or fertilizer or not enough. My sprinkling system breaks whenever a car pulls too close to the edge of the lawn. And I've lost the war against weeds. Sometimes I'm tempted to dynamite the front yard and start over, but that would damage Dad's orange tree.

In my travels across the country and overseas I've visited in many homes and found happy people and miserable people in both small apartments and spacious dwellings, which suggests to me that where we live has little to do with our level of happiness.

Failing to find lasting joy in a house, many people begin to look outside the home to a place where they can "find it all" while they "get away from it all." They plan a dream trip to Hawaii to enjoy the sun and surf or to Colorado to enjoy the snow and skiing. But all too often it's simply that—a dream.

Vacations can be enjoyable, but the possibilities for disaster are endless—bad weather, lost travelers checks, car breakdown, canceled flights, stuffy motel rooms. Our first trip to Hawaii was an illustration of this.

I was to speak in a gorgeous hotel on the north side of Kauai. We looked forward to a week of sunbathing and sightseeing on the island paradise. But it rained every day. The travel brochure conveniently withheld information about the island's average rainfall, which, where we were staying, was 425 inches a year!

Things we least expect can ruin a vacation we've anticipated for months, or even years. Like the time we planned a special ski trip with our relatives. First we lost the key to our shared apartment and nearly froze while we tried to find the manager. Then my niece got a severe nosebleed as we prepared to make our first run down the mountain. And on my second trip down the slope, stomach flu attacked me unexpectedly. As I tried to hide in the woods to relieve my stomach cramps, I slipped and slid forty feet through the trees. My son, Greg, laughed uncontrollably while I spent thirty minutes trying to dig myself out of the snow and clean myself up.

Because I travel so much, people often tell me they envy me; they think traveling is exciting. They do not realize that traveling drills big holes in my cup.

The headache of arranging tickets, rushing to make connections, delayed flights and lost luggage, added to fatigue from jet lag, uncomfortable beds, and flat pillows, drains away any joy that traveling might provide. If you enjoy your family, every day on the road is a day away from those you love most. Most people who look to travel for fulfillment are disappointed.

Places, whether homes or vacation spots, are like a mirage. To a person thirsting for fulfillment, they look like a quenching pool of water. Yet once we reach them we find only sand—and the 10,000 other tourists who beat us to the spot.

POSSESSIONS—WE NEVER GET ENOUGH

If people and places can't satisfy us, perhaps we would be happy if we had more things.

I took a large cut in pay when I parted company with Dale, so I was thrilled when I had a business opportunity that promised to yield at least $200,000 in the first year, and perhaps twice that the following year. Norma and I quickly thought of things we "needed"—a microwave, a new phone system, a sophisticated stereo system, a new washer and dryer. Our house suddenly seemed far too small and outdated. We drove around town and found a beautiful two-story home overlooking a lake. The price was only half of the "minimum" amount we thought I would earn. We began to figure ways to borrow the money for this house in anticipation of our windfall income.

Fortunately the bank never considered our loan request. The amount of money we actually received paid only for those few appliances we bought in anticipation of moving into the new house. Every day those items were a grim reminder that we could not move out of the home we no longer liked.

Money does not provide lasting fulfillment, nor is it the key to the door marked "the overflowing life." I've met as many poor, happy people as I have rich, happy people, and vice versa. Yet many of us live as though cars, campers, and boats bring lasting enjoyment to life.

We see this attitude displayed especially at Christmastime. Millions believe the holiday ad campaigns that tell us which things will bring happiness. But after all the gifts are opened, many of us slide straight into discouragement, even depression. Year after year the pattern repeats itself; new possessions cannot satisfy us for long.

Possessions, like people and places, lose their ability to fulfill us. Trying to quench our thirst from this source is like drinking salty sea water. It shimmers and glistens with promise, but it only leaves us more thirsty and cramped.

If lasting fulfillment is not found in people, places, or possessions, what's left? Disillusioned by these three, many people look to recognition, expecting power or the world's praise to satisfy them.

POSITION—WE CAN NEVER CLIMB HIGH ENOUGH

By the time I started to understand this principle, I had worked in both menial jobs and in what I considered the ultimate in a challenging leadership position for a large corporation. I couldn't imagine going any higher, short of replacing Dale, which I had no desire to do. Yet even at "the top," I finally realized that this position could not provide the continual joy and peace I desired.

Those within the Christian community are not immune. They too fall victim to the myth that they can find fulfillment by achieving position. Some Christians would love to share the limelight with a television personality or be able to sing like their favorite Christian recording artist. Believers in secular jobs may simply long to be able to work for a ministry-related organization or a church. They presume that if they were working in a Christian environment they would not be bothered by the problems and pettiness they find in the secular workplace. Working in that type of environment, they think, would be like having a perpetual "quiet time."

Unfortunately, even in a ministry setting, certain things about work still leave us lacking lasting fulfillment. One reason jobs do not satisfy is that they all have at least one thing in common: *Work!*

Work is not always fun, especially when we have to do the same thing over and over again. Besides, jobs rarely live up to our expectations. When we reach a position for which we've striven, there is usually so much pressure connected with it that it loses much of its glamour. Like owning a big home, the responsibility can consume all our energy.

Most of us focus on what we expect to gain from our job: money, security, promotions, benefits, or fulfillment. We may find these things for a time, but no job is secure. We must continue to perform well or we will lose it. If the company is sold, new management may decide they no longer need us. The economy may slump. The marketplace may change. And all the while we grow older. Nearly all of these factors are beyond our control, but they undermine our position nevertheless.

Les worked thirty-three years as a lineman for the phone company. He thought he had the ultimate in job security. Because of his seniority, he would be one of the last to be laid off; and that was inconceivable because he worked for the largest telephone company in the world—AT&T. Who could have anticipated that Ma Bell would be forced to break up? Only three years away from retirement, Les learned his job would be phased out.

I discovered something interesting while working with professional athletes. Most of us think they enjoy security with their large, multi-year contracts and the glamour of their positions. Instead, however, I often found them disgruntled when they did not perform well, were not playing as often as they felt they deserved to play, were suffering from a nagging injury, or could not get along with their coach. If a contract with a professional sports team is a guarantee of happiness, why do so many professional athletes demand to be traded or to have their contracts renegotiated? And why do they have so many problems with drugs, alcohol, and divorce? No one is immune from the truth that *position* does not provide lasting security and satisfaction.

How many men and women have sacrificed their family life for a higher position only to discover that the position they sought didn't fulfill their expectations? And in the process they lost their relationship with their children. Instead of the fulfillment they were looking for, what did they find? Hurt feelings, anxiety, fear, stress—the very things they were hoping to avoid.

Other areas breed insecurity as well. Many people think they would be fulfilled if they could lead a great cause, work full-time helping people, become a media celebrity, cut a record album, win a political election, or write a book. Consumed by the excitement of these activities, some ignore the potential cost in time or finances, loss of privacy, and demands from supporters.

We need to refocus our expectations on a totally different source. It's not enough to stop expecting fulfillment from people, places, possessions, or position. After my talk with Greg that morning, I realized where *life did not originate.* But I still did not know how to plug into the genuine source of life. I couldn't imagine how or why I had failed to learn such an important truth during my years of seminary, church involvement, or in my association with Dale and his seminars. If I didn't know the answer, who did?

My search for answers began with God Himself. My prayer for help was nothing more than a whimpering cry: "God, teach me what I'm missing. What am I failing to understand?" More than eleven years ago I first prayed that prayer, and I can honestly say that the years since have been the most fulfilling, adventurous, and overflowing I've ever experienced.

Here are three reasons why my cup is full today:

1. Negative emotions such as hurt feelings, envy, jealousy, anger, depression, lust, fear, and worry have virtually faded from my life.
2. Positive, life-giving emotions have replaced negative emotions. I regularly experience love for and from others, and my inner joy and happiness does not depend on God's creation. I have an inner calm and contentment—a peace of mind—that I never used to experience.
3. I've learned how to use the painful, emotionally difficult experiences of life to benefit me and those around me.

A fulfilling life has nothing to do with people, places, possessions, or position. When the true source of fulfillment floods us, a deepening sense of security accompanies it, assuring us that the source of life cannot be yanked away.

Once our cup is filled by this source, we are truly free, for the first time, to enjoy God's creation—because we can appreciate it without depending on it for fulfillment. We live overflowing lives because the *source* of life, instead of the *gifts* of life, brings us contentment. How? By finding the well that never runs dry.

3

Finding the Well
that Never Runs Dry

WHERE WOULD I FIND lasting fulfillment? Learning
that I had looked for contentment in all the wrong
places for so many years left me empty. Even after I
prayed and asked God to show me what was missing,
I felt a hollow darkness inside. Then suddenly, as if
someone switched on emergency flood lights, I began
to realize why I was so discouraged.

It happened in my office on a Monday morning. I had no motivation to begin work and was too
disgusted with Dale to attend the weekly staff meeting. I had just received a letter and a check for sixty
dollars from a minister I had met a few days earlier at
one of our seminars. I reread the letter and felt a wave
of embarrassment. The pastor asked me to use the
money for a new suit. He had noticed that I wore the
same suit for three consecutive years and said his
motivation for sending me the check was 1 John 3:17:
"Whoever has the world's goods, and beholds his
brother in need and closes his heart against him, how

does the love of God abide in him?" How could I explain that I didn't need a new suit? Besides, I probably earned three times his salary. I should have sent him money.

Intrigued by his comments, I reached for my Bible and read the five short chapters of 1 John. Bible reading had become no more than a daily ritual for me during this stress-filled time. For weeks I'd read it without gaining any spiritual insights. But this time my mind was unusually alert as I tried to sense even a hint of truth that might help me. The words in chapter two stunned me: "The one who says he is in the light and *yet* hates his brother is in the darkness until now. The one who loves his brother abides in the light and there is no cause for stumbling in him. But the one who hates his brother is in the darkness and walks in the darkness, and does not know where he is going because the darkness has blinded his eyes" (1 John 2:9–11).

Over and over I read those verses. The word *darkness* precisely described my discouragement and lack of enthusiasm. I knew that walking in God's light meant walking in His love; however, I had never equated my lack of love for Dale with hatred. Maybe others could see it, but I had missed it. Not only did I not love Dale, I had actually developed a deep anger toward him. Left to fester, my anger could have turned into hate.

Could this be true? I felt I was too spiritual and mature to stoop to hating someone. I'd never yelled at Dale or tried to hurt him in any visible way. Yet according to God's Word I was walking in darkness, not in light, because I did not love my brother.

Though perhaps not evident on the outside, my angry thoughts and bitterness proved that inside I hated Dale. And though not affecting him, my hate was destroying me. I could not function in more than the routine activities of my job and life. No wonder I didn't sense God's love or have a desire for spiritual things. I was slipping into darkness and wasn't consciously aware of it.

Rarely has Scripture so overwhelmed me. I slid out of my swivel chair and onto my knees. "God, it's hard for me to admit it, but what You've written in this verse is true of me," I prayed. "Now I understand why I don't sense Your presence and why I'm walking in such confusing darkness."

I left the office knowing my conflict was not with Dale. By allowing anger to remain within me unresolved I was fighting a law of God. Blaming Dale had kept me from seeing my own immaturity and lack of love. In my anger, I had set myself up as his judge. I had examined the evidence and mentally pronounced a guilty verdict. Yet I could not possibly know all the reasons Dale had not followed my recommendations. And even if I had known, by judging him and hating him I was superseding God, the only true judge. I recalled James 4:12: "There is only one . . . judge, the One who is able to save and to destroy; but who are you who judge your neighbor?"

It was time to resolve this. I went home and suggested to Norma that I go away for two or three days to be alone with God. She encouraged me to go, for I'd been impossible to live with. If it would bring me out of my depression, she was eager to give me the time. So I grabbed my Bible, a jug of water, and a pen and paper and headed over to our company's vacant rental house a half mile from our home.

> *During the next two days, I began to learn the secret of having my cup filled to the brim.*

Away from phone, radio, television, and all other interruptions, I spent two days drinking only water, praying, and reading the Gospel of Luke. "Lord," I prayed, "I'm willing to read through this Gospel and as many other books in the Bible as it takes for You to teach me the secret of finding the abundant life You promised."

I spent the entire two days in the Gospel of Luke, though I did refer to other passages of Scripture to confirm what I was learning. Luke 11 was the first chapter to jump out at me. When I read about the disciples asking Jesus to teach them how to pray I thought, *Aha! Maybe this will help me find the answer.* So I prayed, "Lord, teach me how to pray." If I asked God, through prayer, to help me discover the secret to fulfillment, and if He indeed answers prayer, then He would show me the secret I so desperately needed.

The exciting thing about the secret I was about to learn was that it had nothing to do with the people or things around me, or with my position. Furthermore, it had nothing to do with my earthly accomplishments, my level of education, or my financial condition. It had everything to do with understanding Christ's words: "I came that they might have life, and might have it abundantly" (John 10:10).

What I learned from Luke 11 and 18 taught me the greatest secret to life.

DISCOVERING GOD'S BEST

The first clue came in Christ's parable in Luke 11. Can you see in this passage what helped me understand fulfillment?

> And He said to them, "Suppose one of you shall have a friend, and shall go to him at midnight, and say to him, 'Friend, lend me three loaves; for a friend of mine has come to me from a journey, and I have nothing to set before him'; and from inside he shall answer and say, 'Do not bother me; the door has already been shut and my children and I are in bed; I cannot get up and give you anything.' I tell you, even though he will not get up and give him anything because he is his friend, yet because of his *persistence* he will get up and give him as much as he needs. And I say to you, ask, and it shall be given to you; seek, and you shall find; knock, and it shall be opened to you. For everyone who asks, receives; and he who seeks, finds; and to him who knocks, it shall be opened" (Luke 11:5–10).

I acted out this parable in my mind to try to understand it. I pictured myself as the person who went next door to borrow three loaves of bread for my unexpected visitor. I began to knock on my neighbor's door at midnight. "Don't bother us," I heard him shout. "We're all in bed. I can't get up and give you anything." But I knew that if he did not help me I would only have to pass the word around the community the next day and he would be ostracized. My neighbor was a good friend. We'd fished together and shared many meals. Our children played together, and I couldn't say how often we had borrowed things from each other. However, those were not the reasons he eventually helped me at such a late hour. He got up and gave me as much as I needed because of *my persistence and in order to protect his reputation.*

Jesus went on to make the application for us. Why are we to continually ask and seek and knock? *Because God's reputation is at stake.* I could pray, "Lord, what's the secret to the abundant life you promised in John 10:10?" I intended to keep asking this question until I got an answer, and I knew God *would* answer because He will not be shamed. I was asking, and God promised I would receive. I was seeking, and He promised I would find. I was knocking, and He promised to open the door to understanding.

From this parable I learned two crucial principles: First, God will not be shamed. He guards His Word and His reputation as did the neighbor portrayed in the parable I'd read. Second, He is faithful to answer the persistent prayers of His children.

RECOGNIZING GOD'S FAITHFULNESS

As I read the next parable, another truth about prayer emerged.

> Now suppose one of you fathers is asked by his son for a fish; he will not give him a snake instead of a fish, will he? Or if he is asked for an egg, he will not give him a scorpion, will he? If you then, being evil, know how to give good gifts to your children, how much more shall *your* heavenly Father give the Holy Spirit to those who ask Him? (Luke 11:11–13).

If we humans know how to give good gifts to our children, just think about the almighty God of the universe, our heavenly Father. He promises to give His very Spirit to those who ask. I suddenly realized this was what I was seeking. This was the life He had promised! Life was contained in His Spirit living within me. If I had His Holy Spirit, I would have love, joy, peace, patience, and all the other fruit of the Spirit (Galatians 5:22–23). Ephesians 3:19 states that to *know* the love of God is to be "filled up to all the fulness of God." I know it is God's Spirit *alone* that fills my cup.

This wasn't new to me—I'd heard it hundreds of times. What was new was *how* to gain God's Spirit and keep that relationship alive.

During those two days, I went to God as a child goes to his father. As a hungry son seeking bread, I stated my requests:

- I asked to experience Him within me and that I might no longer expect anything other than Him to fill my life.

- I asked for healthy family relationships and that Norma and I and our three children would love each other and be an example to other families.

- I asked for knowledge and wisdom to be the best possible husband and father.

- I asked God for a friend who could guide me further in this truth. I needed someone who would help me resolve my inner turmoil regarding Dale and help me live an obedient Christian life.

- Finally, I asked God to let me guide others, particularly by preparing me to do more personal counseling so I could share my insights from Him.

Even though God promised to be faithful, I couldn't keep myself from making one stipulation. I asked, of all the people who might be that "special friend" to help me grow, that it not be Jim, a most obnoxious older man in Dale's organization. He had a know-it-all attitude so offensive to me that I found it hard to be around him.

The answers to my prayers began almost immediately. First, Dale called me into his office a few days later to discuss how we might resolve the struggle we were having in our relationship. As I stood before him, I wavered as to whether or not I should tell him about all I had been learning and feeling. Just when I was about to open up and express to him what was on my heart, Dale said, "Gary, I think you need to talk to someone besides me about what's been going on. In fact, I've arranged for you to spend a good deal of time with Jim over the next several weeks to talk things out."

Jim! The very person I had prayed I wouldn't have to talk to. I could have resigned on the spot. I was confused and upset with God. I felt as if I had asked for a fish and been given a snake. I couldn't understand why the one person I specifically wanted to avoid was to become a major part of my week.

Though I sensed God's Spirit changing me, I had to struggle to keep from walking out of the room. Yet those two days of prayer and fasting had been so meaningful to me that I prayed instead. "Lord, even though I'm confused and upset, I am not going to try to figure this out. I'm willing to let You prove Your faithfulness in my life."

That afternoon I started meeting with Jim, and almost overnight God used him to pull me further out of my discouragement. Instead of the pride-filled, know-it-all I expected to find, Jim was caring and compassionate. More than I ever thought possible, he understood Dale as well as my conflict with Dale. Instead of lecturing me, he listened and prayed with me. In the time I spent with Jim over the next few weeks my attitude changed from resentment at having to meet with him to feeling rewarded because we were meeting.

This was a major turning point. I began to realize that God was not giving me a scorpion or a snake. He was faithful in answering my prayer. Yet like a loving Father, He knew what I truly needed. I could relax and trust Him even when I didn't understand what He was doing. My confidence in God grew by leaps and bounds as I continued to knock on His door for my other requests.

God had answered my prayer about finding a close friend to help me work through the situation with Dale, and soon I began receiving answers to my other requests as well. I had prayed to be a godly husband and father and to learn to keep my family in harmony. Without me lifting a finger, God answered that prayer by opening up a door to a ministry I never expected to have any part in.

A good friend and pastor I had met through our business called and asked if I would consider doing three things in his church: First, he wanted me to become a better husband and father so I could teach others out of my own life experiences. Second, he wanted me to develop a ministry to families. And third, he asked me to begin a counseling program at his church.

While Norma and I prayed about this exciting opportunity, an almost identical offer came from another pastor in California. Now I had not only one chance to learn about my family and family ministry, but two!

This dilemma fascinated me, and I've seen it happen many times since. God is so faithful that He often gives several answers to a single request. Those two offers showed me how far I had slipped into discouragement. Before getting into the Gospel of Luke, I had questioned whether I would ever see any answers to prayer or to life and whether I would ever be of any service to God. These opportunities showed me that our ways are never hidden from the Lord and that regardless of our circumstances, He has a task for us to accomplish for Him.

Seeing the things I had prayed for come together reassured me of God's faithfulness. I hadn't sent out dozens of résumés looking for a job, nor had I asked Jim to become my friend. Yet in both cases God, in His own way and timing, had honored my requests, just as He said He would in Luke 11.

Norma and I decided to accept the first offer—to serve as a family pastor at a growing church—and we prepared to move our family to another state. As I began to plan my departure from Dale's company, I felt a renewed love for the people I was leaving. Even though my conflict with Dale had been devastating in many ways, I found I still loved him and knew, finally, that God had used our problems to bring me closer to Him. In fact, I began to understand that if I had never gone through that experience I might never have discovered the depth of God's faithfulness nor become so meaningfully related to Him.

But God had taught me another truth concerning prayer that has become my primary tool for finding answered prayer.

PERSISTENCE—A SECRET TO ANSWERED PRAYER

During the two days I camped out in the Book of Luke, I listened intently each time Jesus spoke about prayer. In Luke 18 Jesus introduced two parables by telling His disciples that "they ought to pray and not lose heart" (v. 1). The first story He used is now one of my favorites; in it lies a fantastic secret to effective prayer. Here's the scene:

Imagine an unrighteous, wicked judge assigned to a small city in Israel. He has no respect for God or man. He is disgruntled because He would rather be in Rome enjoying pageantry, games, and parties. Instead he's stuck with a bunch of farmers, shepherds, and religious fanatics. Every day people line up to present their grievances to him and he passes judgments according to his mood.

In the line of people stands a widow with no one to look out for her best interests or to protect her. Her situation appears hopeless. Others take advantage of her, but she has no legal rights. Although many look at her as helpless, she knows the secret to gaining justice. The first time she presents her petition to the judge, he brusquely dismisses her. But she does not give up. After coming before him repeatedly, she finally gains legal protection, "lest by continually coming she wear me out" the judge decides (Luke 18:5).

Jesus said to listen carefully to the story of this unrighteous judge. He pictures an important truth people need to understand. It was the woman's persistence that brought results. Jesus goes on to say,

"Shall not God bring about justice for His elect, who cry to Him day and night, and *will He delay long over them*?" (Luke 18:7).

Following my two-day retreat, I imagined myself coming every day as the widow did and lining up before God. From chapter 11, I learned God was loving and that He would be faithful to His children. From chapter 18, I learned to get in God's prayer line every day, a practice I have continued since 1975.

When I line up to pray, my petitions fall into three categories: First, I ask for what God promises to give His children—love, joy, and peace through His Holy Spirit—that's fulfillment. Second, I pray about the needs of my family. And third, I pray for the needs of people around me.

After we moved away from Dale and his business, one of my major needs was to be free of resentment toward him. I knew it was wrong for me to feel betrayed and to desire revenge, but I could not shake myself loose from these emotions. Every day for two years I applied the principle from the parable in Luke 18 and prayed as I jogged: "Lord, I'm in line again, along with many of Your children. I must admit how upset I still am with Dale. I don't know how You're going to do it, but I know You're going to free me. Maybe this is the day! And if not today, perhaps tomorrow!"

After two years of getting in line every day and requesting that freedom, it finally came. A man from my church approached me with an article from a counseling magazine. "This article describes a problem I'm having," he said. "Would you read it and then could we talk about how to solve my problem?"

Even though this man was looking for help for his own problem, the article perfectly described *my* conflict with Dale. It also provided the final pieces of information I needed to resolve it completely.

The article explained that much of Dale's strong drive to achieve came from several conflicts he had never resolved, especially his father's overpowering emphasis on success as measured by how much he produced. Acceptance from his parents came only when he overachieved. In addition, Dale felt compelled to use people to reach his overachieving goals. When they didn't help him achieve, he discarded them, which explained why I was only one in a trail of broken relationships Dale had suffered. Finally I saw why he couldn't repair his own broken relationships.

I also learned that real forgiveness required my prayers and actions to release Dale from the grip of overachieving inner conflict. Dale was crippled by always having to gain approval. Why should I be angry with him? He needed understanding. I needed to love and help him instead of draining away all my emotional energy by being bitter toward him. Once I stopped long enough to *understand* Dale, I was finally able to forgive him. That day I stepped out of that prayer line and never again needed to get back in it. My resentment toward Dale never returned.

Shortly after reading that article, and after God released me from my anger, I drove to one of Dale's health seminars and had a great visit with him. Some of the things that once made me angry reappeared, but this time, rather than bristling and wanting to separate myself from him, I listened and felt genuine love for Dale and respect for his work. I actually wanted to pray for a special blessing of God on his life. That's when I knew I was really free! In fact, we continue to see each other and talk on the phone. I realize now that my problem with Dale was not Dale's problem. It was my attitude.

God not only is faithful to answer our persistent prayers for spiritual needs but for physical needs as well. An example of God's faithfulness in taking care of everyday practical concerns involved my daughter Kari. Every night for approximately two years the two of us stood in line asking God to provide a car. I was earning significantly less than I had with Dale, and our family station wagon was on its last legs and full of rattles. The engine was unreliable, and I had rewired the broken springs in the front seat on the driver's side with coat hangers. I did not have the money to replace the car and did not want to go into debt again, but I never mentioned the need to anyone else.

One afternoon while working with a businessman, we took a break for a hamburger and he decided to drive my car. When he sank down in the seat and leaned toward the door he asked if this was my only car. I said it was. "This is pathetic," he said. I laughed and agreed with him, but was caught totally by surprise by what he said next. "Tomorrow I want you to go down to any car lot in town and pick any car you want. I'll pay for it."

That kind of experience has been repeated again and again in all areas of need. I never presume on God's timing, and I never expect satisfaction from any material thing He gives. Yet time after time His provisions for my physical needs remind me that God is indeed my source of life. Even with things like misplacing my wallet or keys, it's fun to get in line and watch Him resolve the "little" things.

What's exciting about all this is that any child of God can experience the joy of trusting Him. I've learned that I can't take pride in what He does for me because it is His faithfulness, not my spirituality, that makes the difference.

DEPENDING ON GOD FOR LASTING LIFE

Humbled, alert, and convicted, I became child-like, completely dependent on Christ for both life and direction, the exact position He wanted me in. But many of us have a hard time believing God cares so deeply for us.

I once met a woman in counseling who didn't think she could depend on God in the same way she used to depend on her doting father. Sherie was single, 36 years old, and with tears she challenged God and me. "You say God loves me and can meet all of my needs and fill my cup," she said. "But who's going to take care of me? Who's going to talk to me? Who's He providing for me?" Then she added, "I have a car stereo that won't fit my car. It was a gift so I can't return it, and I don't even know the first thing to do about it. Now tell me how God can meet a need like that?"

I did not know how God would meet her

needs, but I knew He could, even with her stereo. "Are you willing to ask God to become the source of your life and to depend on Him for every need?" I asked her. At first she couldn't do it because she still felt God had cheated her. We got on our knees and with tears she prayed, "God, I want to depend on you, but I can't." After two more tries, she finally blurted out, "Okay, God, I will completely trust my life in Your hands and let You, in Your timing, fill my life and take care of my everyday needs."

That encounter left her emotionally exhausted, and I honestly did not expect much to happen for a while. But the next morning she could hardly wait to call me. She had called a retailer to see if she could exchange her stereo. The store manager said he didn't carry that model but suggested that she call the factory office. She did. It was after working hours, so a regional manager answered the phone. After some discussion, he recognized her name. Her father had been one of his closest friends in high school. "If you're his daughter," he said, "I'll take complete care of whatever you need."

Stunned, Sherie recognized this as a demonstration of God's faithfulness. In subsequent years, she has filled several notebooks detailing how God has met her specific needs.

Some people may object, saying that everyone experiences similar "coincidences" and that they aren't necessarily from God. Maybe it's not an important question for the small things in life, but when people ask God for fulfillment, peace, joy, and love, and they come in lasting amounts, that's worth shouting about. And aren't those our deepest needs? God is faithful to provide what we need when we get in His line. In the same way a child asks a parent for candy or a new toy, we can petition God for the "small things." If He doesn't give them, perhaps they aren't really needs. But He will fulfill His specific promises, such as those for abundant life (John 10:10) and inner peace (John 14:27).

A FINAL LESSON ON PRAYER

In Luke 18:18–30 Jesus spoke the words that became the basis for the famous quote of Jim Elliott, the missionary to the Auca Indians who was martyred in Ecuador: "A man is no fool who gives up what he cannot keep to gain what he will never lose."

Christ promised His disciples in Luke 18:29–30 that anyone who seeks God's kingdom above home, mate, brothers, sisters, parents, and children will receive many times more *at this time* as well as eternal life in the age to come. But how does putting God first help us in our everyday problems?

Like many of us, Donna needed to learn to put God first in everyday living. She progressed from anger to hatred to apathy toward her husband, Dave, because of an affair he'd had. She was so disgusted that she did not speak to him for days. Donna was surprised when her pastor showed her that her hatred and judgmental attitude were wrong in God's eyes. Until she saw the log in her own eye, she could not possibly help her husband. Donna humbled herself by admitting her own sin. She also learned to pray for her husband and to wait on God to change him.

Over the next several days, a new love for her husband and a previously unknown sense of calm seeped into Donna's soul. She even started doing special things for him. As the weeks went by, Dave noticed the change in her behavior. Captivated by the beauty of her peacefulness, he finally broke down and asked what had happened. When Donna confessed her judgmental spirit and explained her new dependency on God, Dave expressed his desire for the same peace and joy. Together they went back to the pastor, who helped Dave discover what Donna had found. They became one of the most radiant couples in our church, all because Donna escaped from the darkness of her anger and began walking in the light of her new dependency on God. She saw the truth, grabbed hold of it, and found lasting fulfillment in knowing God personally.

In addition to having my life completely filled, I still enjoy the pleasures of knowing and serving people, of traveling to new places, of having some possessions, and of gaining some position. But these things are no longer what I look to for fulfillment; they are simply the overflow.

> *If I lost them all I would still be full because I have the source of life itself—a personal relationship with Jesus Christ (1 John 5:11–12).*

I once heard a story about a man who died and was given a guided tour of heaven by St. Peter. When they came to an immense warehouse filled with all shapes and sizes of wrapped packages, the man asked Peter what they were. Peter replied sadly, "This is where God keeps all the gifts He intended for His children. These were never claimed." Unfortunately, many today never claim God's promised packages. We leave His gifts in the warehouse of heaven, either because we never ask or because we get out of line too soon.

I do not want anyone to miss out on God's gifts the way I did for so many years, especially the gift of life itself. This new life overflows with meaning so satisfying that the thrill of other pursuits is as fleeting as the momentary excitement of an amusement park ride.

4

Grabbing Hold of Fulfillment

NEVER UNDERESTIMATE the power of a woman who has yielded her life to God. She not only has strength, but a special, radiating beauty. Norma had that glow during our courtship and when we were first married. After several years of marriage, however, her power and beauty started to fade, and she blamed me for her lack of fulfillment.

Norma was frustrated with me for good reason. Before my crisis with Dale, I traveled nearly fifty percent of the time and was so consumed with my work that I had little energy left for her and the kids. When Michael, our third child, was born, he was sick much of the time and so Norma could not maintain the house and care for the children without my help.

She tried conventional methods to get me to change. She talked to me, she pleaded, she cried. Nothing worked. I didn't change, and neither did she.

But then Norma tried something *unconventional.* Her action motivated me to go to Dale and ask for a different position in the company so I could spend more time at home.

What was this powerful action she took?

> *Norma quit fighting. She realized she wasn't fighting me; she was fighting God's plan for fulfillment.*

Norma had read about God's love for her. He had demonstrated His love by sending Jesus Christ, His only Son, to give her abundant life. By demanding that I change, she was in essence saying that she could not experience a full life unless God somehow used me to meet her needs. But God was ready and willing to meet her needs, apart from me, if she would only let Him.

With no coaching from me, Norma changed her thinking, admitted she hadn't been seeking God alone, and began her own journey to find God's fulfilling love. Rather than complain to me, she prayed, "Lord, thank You that all I need is You. You know I want a good relationship with Gary and that I want him to spend more time at home. You also know that I'm not very strong physically. I'm so tired that I don't feel I can last much longer under this strain. I'm coming to You with these requests because I know that if I *need* Gary at home, *You* can either make it happen or take away my desire. I'm going to stop fighting Gary and instead ask You either to change him or to meet my needs in some other way."

To find God's fulfillment, Norma took steps

similar to those I later discovered. She stopped expecting life from me and started looking to God. She realized I not only would not, but could not, fill her life, so she went to the source of life and asked Him to fill her.

The results were startling. I noticed the change almost immediately. When I came home from work, I sensed a calm spirit in our house. Norma's face was peaceful, no longer tense. Instead of the usual harsh words, her conversation was quiet and she was more interested in asking me how my day had gone than in relating her activities with the children.

After a few days, I couldn't keep from asking what had happened. "Gary, I got tired of fighting you," she explained calmly. "I realized that I wasn't trusting God concerning our marriage and family, and so I decided to stop complaining and start praying. I've told God that I would like you to spend more time at home, and if I really need that, I know He will make the necessary changes." She also grabbed my attention by stating, in a calm and undemanding way, "I think I'm headed for a physical collapse. Michael has been sick so much, and with all the other responsibilities, I don't think I can last much longer."

Imagine what that did to me. I was instantly convicted that my priorities were wrong. And that wasn't all. Because Norma had changed, I *wanted* to spend more time at home. That same week I asked Dale to change my job so I could spend more time meeting my family's needs.

What Norma did summarizes the first three

chapters. She stopped looking to people, places, possessions, and position and turned to a trustworthy God Who answers the persistent prayers of His children. He promises life, and He delivers!

Some may think Norma just disguised her selfishness by asking God to change me instead of nagging me to change. I disagree. I encourage wives to ask God for a good relationship with their husbands and children. That request is not selfish. A good relationship benefits not only the wife, but the entire family, the Christian community, and ultimately our nation and the entire world. It also glorifies God, because a godly marriage is a picture of our relationship with Christ (Ephesians 5:22–23).

Once we're into the habit of seeking fulfillment from the world, we won't learn overnight to look to God as the source of life. It took Norma and me several years before looking to the Lord was our natural, first response, and at times we still catch ourselves focusing on someone or something other than Him.

The procedure we follow is not magic. Neither does it need to be kept legalistically like a scientific formula. These are simply guidelines we have followed that we hope you can learn from and adapt to your unique situation. God creates us as individuals, not as carbon copies, so put your own fingerprints on the steps that follow.

STEP OUT OF FANTASYLAND

Many Christians, frustrated by the lack of fulfillment they've found in people, places, possessions, and position, have fallen for the deception that God's Word is not entirely true. They live as though the Bible were a book of myths rather than a living and active guide to fulfillment. For them, the hope of gaining lasting love, joy, and peace is like believing Disneyland is real. And attending church is like the temporary thrill of one of Disney's rides. Behind the splashing water, flashing lights, dark tunnels, and dancing figures are only computers and wires and sophisticated sound systems. Christianity is a make-believe world, a ride they take Sunday after Sunday. It doesn't satisfy, but they keep riding because deep down they want to believe it is real.

Others, looking for a greater thrill, switch to different rides, like a new church, a different speaker, or some new teaching. The new ride is more exciting at first, but no more satisfying in the long run.

Some have quit taking the rides altogether. They are convinced that those who say they find fulfillment in the Lord lack depth and settle for the simplistic solutions found in a make-believe world.

How do we escape the amusement park syndrome where rides go nowhere except up and down, round and round? We begin by admitting that we have sought fulfillment from people, places, possessions, or positions. These four P's describe our personal Disneyland. The entrance to this amuse-ment park is wide, and many go through it. But Christ said the gate that leads to life is narrow and only a few find it.

The call to hand over tickets we've paid a high price for is difficult to obey, but that's the requirement. It's called confession. We must admit we've been standing in the wrong line and step willingly into God's line.

STEP INTO TRUTH

Admitting we've been in the wrong line is only the first step toward reality. We also need to move into the right line. That is what the Bible means by repentance. It's stepping out of one line and into another. It's turning away from one way of thinking and embracing God's way. It's changing directions, rejecting our former source of expectations and accepting a new source, one that will never fail.

How does this concept actually work? Here's an example in an area where many of us struggle—society's emphasis on sexual "freedom." From toothpaste to cars to flowers to resort hotels, we can hardly buy anything that a sparsely dressed woman has not advertised. Because our society is obsessed with sex, lust is a major temptation.

Even though I had a very rewarding relationship with Norma, I was not immune from this temptation. I met a woman at work whom I found very attractive. Through months of periodic contact, I gradually developed a strong emotional attachment to her. As I gained her confidence she began to tell me some personal struggles she was having. I empathized with her and wanted to take her in my arms and comfort her. When I was honest, I knew I really wanted more than that. But holding her would be enough, I told myself.

During those weeks of temptation I was also learning that people cannot give ultimate meaning to my life. At times I desired to be with this woman, but whenever my thoughts strayed I would confess that she was not the source of my life and admit that I was standing in the wrong line. Then I would ask God to make me realize that what appeared to be as harmless and fun as an amusement park ride was actually a real-life thrill ride that would crash at the end.

Once I had confessed my desire to have someone other than Christ fill my life, I would get back into the line that leads to knowing Him personally. Although I didn't know it at the time, the Lord was teaching me an important principle about "staying in His line" during times of temptation.

RETURN TO THE SOURCE OF JOY

Once we have switched lines, how do we continue to experience this gift of life? The apostle Paul writes in 1 Thessalonians 5:16, "Rejoice always." In Philippians 4:4 he commands, "Rejoice in the Lord always; again I will say, rejoice!" Paul is so emphatic about this because the word "rejoice" literally means "return to the source of our joy."

In the case of this other woman, I obeyed Paul's instruction to rejoice by praying, "Lord, You know, and I'm just discovering, that this girl will never fill my cup. If anything, she could drill huge holes in it. Not only would I probably wind up in disharmony with her (that's usually the case with couples who've had affairs), it would undoubtedly do tremendous damage to my family and to Your reputation. But the most foolish result of all would be that I would cut myself off from You, the very source of life. So right this moment, Lord, I'm asking You to fill my cup. Thank You for letting me see this before it's too late. However long it takes, I will stay in Your line until I'm free from her and filled with You."

Over the years a similar prayer of rejoicing has kept me, in many situations, from giving in to such temptations as envy, jealousy, fear, and anger. Rejoicing, even in times of testing, is acknowledging that God is the source of life. And rejoicing brings us to the place where our lives can be filled by the source of life—God Himself.

Ephesians 3:14–21 is the best explanation of rejoicing I have found.

> For this reason, I bow my knees before the Father, from whom every family in heaven and on earth derives its name, that He would grant you, according to the riches of His glory, to be strengthened with power through His Spirit in the inner man; so that Christ may dwell in your hearts through faith; and that you, being rooted and grounded in love, may be able to comprehend with all the saints what is the breadth and length and height and depth, and to know the love of Christ which surpasses knowledge, *that you may be filled up to all the fulness of God.* Now to Him who is able to do exceeding abundantly beyond all that we ask or think, according to the power that works within us, to Him be the glory

in the church and in Christ Jesus to all genera-
tions forever and ever. Amen.

Note the italicized words: *That you may be
filled up to all the fulness of God.* That is God's desire
and gift to us. And in the next verse, Paul talks about
Him who is able to do *exceeding abundantly beyond
all that we ask or think. That's the overflow—the
exciting, fulfilling life we all desire. It's waiting for us.
We can experience it by rejoicing.*
Rejoicing begins when we acknowledge that
God is the source of all life. In fact, He *is* life, which is
why we can adore Him and sing praise to Him.
Rejoicing reveals faith, because it demonstrates our
expectation that God will reveal to us the depths and
heights of His love. All of this is so that we may be
filled up to all *the fulness of God.* The ultimate in
fulfillment.

MAKE GOD YOUR BEST FRIEND

During my time of temptation, I learned that
the principle of rejoicing was reliable. Simply going to
the source of joy and getting to know Him personally
as my very best friend filled my life. Christ wants to be
our friend. He said we are His friends *if* we obey His
command to love Him and each other. Obeying Him
does not mean I am like a slave. He says in John 15:15,
"No longer do I call you slaves; for the slave does not
know what his master is doing; but I have called you
friends, for all things that I have heard from My Father
I have made known to you."
Most of us have enjoyed a close friendship.

When we're with that friend, we're relaxed and free to be ourselves. We enjoy each other's company. I believe rejoicing—returning to each other often—is the key to fruitful friendship. That's why making God our very best friend is the way to lasting joy. To experience God's joy on a daily basis we must become His friend.

I picture myself like the widow standing in God's line, waiting patiently for Him to meet my inner spiritual needs and my family's material needs. I do this while I run every morning. During the half hour to an hour that I'm pounding the road, I enjoy a special, uninterrupted time of building a meaningful friendship with Christ.

Each person must find the time that is right for him or her. It might be while eating or dressing. During quiet moments of Bible reading and prayer. While driving to and from work. While ironing, cooking, or washing dishes. During a break at work. The important thing is that we not let the cares and pressures of everyday living squeeze out our daily personal time with the source of life.

In addition to spending time alone with God, we must also spend time in His Word. Reading God's Word is essential for getting to know His thoughts. In fact, spending time in His Word plugs us into the source of life. In John 6:63 Jesus says, "The words that I have spoken to you are spirit and are life." And in John 17:17 Jesus prays to the Father on behalf of His disciples saying, "Sanctify them in the truth; Thy word is truth."

There is a very important balance between

knowing Christ and knowing *about* Him. Neither worshiping the Bible nor ignoring it can bring steady spiritual growth. Reading God's Word and not developing a personal relationship with Him is like reading a biography of President Reagan but never getting to know him.

But Christ and the Word are one (John 1:1), so it is impossible to know Him without knowing His Word. And the only way to have an intimate friendship with Him is to communicate with Him, to let His words sink into our souls.

I can understand this better when I think in terms of my relationship with Norma, who is my very best friend. One of the reasons we are so close is because we have security in our relationship through consistent communication, a sharing of our deepest emotions, a communion of our spirits, and regular, meaningful touching. My friendship with Norma helps me know God better as a friend.

Friendship with God is also security. The apostle Paul mentions that security in Romans 8:38–39: "For I am convinced that neither death, nor life, nor angels, nor principalities, nor things present, nor things to come, nor powers, nor height, nor depth, nor any other created thing, shall be able to separate us from the love of God, which is in Christ Jesus our Lord." Just as I'm committed to Norma, I'm committed to God for life, and I know He's committed to me.

Friendship with God is prayer. Just as we cannot know a friend without communicating, we cannot know God without regular conversation with

Him through prayer. Prayer is a two-way street. I express my love, devotion, and feelings, and I listen to Him as well. The closer the friendship, the more intimate our sharing. One of the reasons King David knew God so well was because he poured out his emotions in verse after verse in Psalms and contrasted his feelings with the awesome greatness of God. "How precious also are Thy thoughts to me, O God! How vast is the sum of them! If I should count them, they would outnumber the sand. When I awake, I am still with Thee" (Psalm 139:17–18).

Friendship with God is identification. True friendship requires a willingness to be seen together. A person is not truly a friend unless we are willing to be identified with that person. This is one reason communion and baptism are so important, and why physical signs such as kneeling, singing, and other forms of worship reflect our relationship with God.

Friendship with God is dependency. One of the benefits of knowing God as our friend is being able to express our physical and material needs to Him. When we seek to know God, we are promised that our material needs will be met (Matthew 6:33), but we need to remind ourselves constantly that having our physical needs met will not give us life. Life comes only through knowing God, not from the material goods He gives us.

Friendship with God is gratefulness. An important element of a good friendship is mutual admiration, which is another way of saying we should not take each other for granted. We need to be grateful for the friendship, and sometimes we need to express our gratefulness in tangible ways.

By realizing how faithful God has been and wants to be to those who draw close to Him, we can develop a grateful, thankful heart even before we receive answers to our prayers. Paul tells us in Philippians 4:6 to "Be anxious for nothing, but in everything by prayer and supplication *with thanksgiving* let your requests be made known to God." The next verse confirms how God fills our cup. The *peace* of God, which surpasses all of our comprehension, protects our hearts and our minds in Christ Jesus.

During my time of praying about my lust, I was able to thank God for freeing me even *before* He did because I knew He would be faithful and that I would not get out of His line until He helped me. It was His will that I be faithful to His commands and to the wife He gave me, so I was confident that He would answer my prayer for mental and physical purity.

One of the benefits of expressing gratefulness is contentment in knowing that God will fill my cup and provide for my needs. The same spirit that Paul describes in Philippians 4:11 has become mine, for I too have learned the secret of being content in whatever circumstances I am in.

Also, like the great King David, my inner calm and peace continues as I follow his example in Psalm 62. My soul no longer expects anything from God's creation but waits in silence for God only. I command my soul to do the same thing David did: "Wait in silence for God only, for my hope is from Him. He only is my rock and my salvation, my stronghold; I shall not be shaken. On God my salvation and my glory rest; the rock of my strength, my refuge is in

God" (vv. 5–7). I have determined to trust Him at all times and to wait for His faithfulness.

DECIDE TO BE FILLED

The feelings associated with gratefulness and contentment may take time to develop. Contentment results from *deciding* to rest in the faithfulness of God. Calmness results from *seeing* His faithfulness time after time. I meet many discouraged Christians who experience little of God's faithfulness because they get out of His line too soon. They don't allow God to answer in His perfect timing. Because they are discouraged, they don't feel like getting back into line. It's a defeating cycle, but we can choose to break it.

Our decision to rest in God's faithfulness can be based on the promises clearly given in Scripture. God promises to be our rock, shield, rear guard, shepherd, king, rescuer, hiding place, living water, bread of life, light, physician, our life-supplying vine, our power to overcome sin, our advocate before the Father, our free gift of eternal life, as well as our source of wisdom, joy, peace, love, and self-control. The list goes on and on.

These promises are facts, given to God's people who stand in His line like the widow in Luke 18. Gratefulness, praise, wonder, and excitement can become real as we witness His work in our lives. The faithful, trustworthy fact, according to His Word, is that He provides these emotions to all who love Him.

The process of discovering and knowing Jesus Christ as the source of life can continue every day for the rest of our lives. Getting to know Christ gives life richness, for we can never fully know the depth of His love. Every day is an opportunity to see a new dimension. Unfortunately that doesn't mean we never get sidetracked or discouraged. The false promises of the world in which we live continually draw us away from the source of life.

Negative emotions also draw us away from God. Anger, loneliness, and hurt feelings can make us feel as if God has deserted us or let us down. Actually, the opposite is true. God allows these feelings to help us see where our expectations are focused, whether on God or on His creation. In the next chapter we will find out how to use negative emotions as an early warning system, alerting us that we need to return to the source of life, which is Christ Jesus Himself.

5

Discovering the Main Cause of Unhappiness

JIM HAD BEEN comfortably married for almost ten years, and he and his wife had a healthy, though somewhat unexciting, relationship. Jim had never been the type to send cards or flowers, but this year he wanted to do something special for his wife on their anniversary. He asked his secretary what he could do to show his wife he really loved her.

"Flowers," she said. "Send flowers. And buy her a big box of candy as well. In fact, you might even find a romantic poem, memorize it, and recite it to her when you give her the gifts."

Inspired by his secretary's suggestions, Jim canceled his afternoon appointments, drove to the florist and to the candy store, and even stopped at the library and found a book of poems. Nearly bursting with excitement, Jim drove to his house, carried his pile of presents to the front door, and rang the doorbell. When his wife answered the door, Jim started to recite the poem he had selected and handed her the candy and flowers.

His wife stared at him for a moment and then began to cry.

"What's the matter?" Jim asked.

"What's the matter?" his wife sobbed. "The garage door opener broke this morning; the baby has been sick and is running from both ends; the dog ate the remote control for the television; and now you come home drunk!"

In this make-believe story, the response Jim received from his wife was the opposite of what he expected. The same thing happens in real life. At one time or another all of us will be in situations in which our expectations are unfulfilled, and unfulfilled expectations are a primary cause of negative emotions and unhappiness. Many people who struggle with negative emotions actually use them as weapons against themselves. Every day, people make statements like, "How could I have gotten so angry at my wife?" or "I can't believe she got that raise. I know I shouldn't feel this way, but . . . " or "For six years I've been dating him. I can't believe it's over."

Many of us deny and try to push away these painful feelings. But consider this:

Anger, hurt feelings, fear, and lust can actually help us develop a closer, more vital relationship with Christ.

That statement may sound incredible because negative emotions are usually associated with a lack of spiritual maturity and unhappiness. And it's true, allowed to fester and develop, they can draw us away from God. We have all seen numerous examples of how the "deeds of the flesh" (Galatians 5:19) can hurt and damage relationships. But as Christians, we need not become victims of our emotions. Even negative emotions can be the impetus that moves us back to the source of joy.

We can never completely avoid negative emotions; we will all experience anger and fear and loneliness on occasion. The issue is how often we have them and how we use them. There are many ways to respond to negative emotions; some ways are healthy, others are not.

An unhealthy response to negative emotions is to try and stuff them deep inside or pretend they don't exist. The damage of denying our emotions is well illustrated by the story of a Spartan boy in ancient Greece. At the age of seven the boy left home to begin a life-long career of harsh military service. He was taught every aspect of military combat. He learned survival skills and was taught to hide every trace of emotion.

One day the boy captured a fox and was playing with the animal when he saw his instructor approach him. Quickly he stuffed the wild fox underneath his cloak. In keeping with their custom, the teacher questioned the boy at length. The boy calmly responded to the teacher's endless questions, his face never betraying a hint of pain or fear even though the fox was gnawing and tearing at his unprotected body. Finally, suffering from mortal wounds, the boy fell dead at his teacher's feet. He became the model of Spartan discipline, and this story was later used as an example of genuine manhood. Yet those "manly" qualities killed him.

Some Christians view such control of their emotions as a measure of spirituality. No matter how much they are struggling or hurting, they believe they must always present a facade of happiness.

The model Christ gave us, however, was not that of a spartan. Jesus wept at the grave of a friend. He became angry at the money changers in the temple. He was even accused of being a "wine-bibber" and a "glutton" because he attended a wedding and other parties. Denying negative emotions may leave us looking good on the outside, but it can be destroying us on the inside.

A second option is to allow our emotions to run their natural course with the attitude that there's nothing we can do about them. The problem with unchecked emotions, however, is that they can harm others as well as ourselves. Ken and Cindy are an example.

Ken came from a home where everything was always clean and neat; Cindy's family wasn't as concerned about neatness. This difference created a great deal of conflict in their marriage. When Cindy was tired after a hard day's work, she let the housework wait until another day. This frustrated Ken, who constantly fired verbal darts at his wife: "What are these clothes doing in the corner?" "This room looks like the dust bowl." "You expect the ants to clean these dishes?"

One morning Cindy awoke to hear Ken vacuuming the living room at six o'clock. She staggered out of the bedroom and asked what he was doing. "I'm sick and tired of living in this pigpen!" he yelled. Ken's outburst of anger and his degrading comments left Cindy defeated and destroyed her motivation to change. But Ken seemed unaware of the damage his anger caused his wife. Venting his negative emotions made Ken feel better for the moment, but it caused lasting scars in his relationships.

Releasing pent-up emotions may be considered good therapy in some circles, but it comes at a high price. A friend who worked at a psychiatric hospital relayed the tragic story of Brian. Brian had a great deal of anger at what he considered unfair actions his parents had taken. As part of Brian's therapy he was put into a room with an inflated BoBo doll, which was to be used as a punching bag. "Just pretend this doll is your parents," Brian was told, "and use it to release all your hostilities."

After destroying two BoBo dolls Brian fell to the floor in exhaustion. His therapy was termed a success, but when he was released from the hospital a month later he returned home and crippled his father in a fit of rage. Neither denying nor venting our emotions is the answer.

For Christians, another option is available.

Those who know Christ can use negative emotions as warning signals.

Ken looked at Cindy as the cause of his anger without recognizing that his anger revealed his problem as well.

If Ken had been willing, he could have harnessed the power of his anger to draw him closer to God—even to make him more loving. How is this possible? If we recognize that negative emotions are like warning lights on the dashboard of a car, we can use them to warn us that we are headed for trouble.

Imagine that you are driving me to the airport after I have spoken in your city. We're enjoying a fascinating discussion when suddenly I notice a red light flashing on your dash, warning you that the car is overheating. When I draw your attention to the light, you tell me to ignore it. "It always flashes on and off," you say.

After several miles of traveling with the red light on, I once again mention my concern. "OK, OK," you say, "open up the glove compartment and give me a hammer, will you?" I do as you ask, and then, with a smile, you smash the light. "There," you say, "that should make you feel better. Now will you quit pestering me?"

Three miles later the car comes to a halt in a blanket of smoke, and I miss my plane. Because you failed to admit the reality of the problem and acknowledge the warning light, you must now deal with my frustration and your own embarrassment.

Although this story is exaggerated, I regularly see people doing this very thing in counseling. They come to me with warning lights flashing in their lives, but instead of using the valuable information the lights could provide, they ignore or smash them.

Probably the most important thing that negative emotions reveal—and certainly the most destructive—is our own self-centeredness. Just how self-centered are we? I asked a beautiful model that question several years ago.

Mary came to my office and asked for help in her struggles with her husband. As I listened to her complain about his harsh, demanding, and insensitive ways, I noticed that her face reflected a hard, deep-seated resentment. She spent a great deal of time describing his lack of love. He demanded that she dress in a certain way so he would always look good with her. Once when she scratched the car fender he treated her like a child by taking her "toy" away until she "learned how to drive."

She left herself wide open when she paused to say, "I'm really hurting over my husband's treatment. Is there anything I can do to relieve the pain?" This was early in my ministry and today I would probably not use such a bold approach. I forced Mary to face something she didn't want to face when I asked her, "How self-centered do you think you are?"

First amazement, then irritation at my brash question spread across her face. "I'm not very self-centered at all," she responded. "Most of my time is spent taking care of the children or my husband. I have almost no time for myself."

Not sure where this would lead, I asked Mary if I could give her some homework. Her assignment was to write down every time she was angry or had hurt feelings and to ask herself *what she was personally losing* that might cause hurt or anger. She agreed to return in a week and share the results.

During our next appointment Mary confessed that for the first time she realized how many things she unconsciously expected of her husband, her children, and her environment. She had filled three pages with incidents and discovered that every time she was angry or hurt, someone was denying her something she wanted. When I asked her again how self-centered she thought she was she lowered her head as she answered, "*Very* self-centered." I immediately confessed that I too was self-centered and that it was a toss-up as to who was more selfish. But I probably had her beat.

Admitting we are selfish is not easy. I like to be thought of as a caring, compassionate, giving person who always looks out for the best interests of others. But in reality, my best attempts to be righteous are as filthy rags, according to the prophet Isaiah (Isaiah 64:6).

We all need to admit our level of self-centeredness because out of such an admission comes the freedom to refocus our expectations away from God's creation and onto God.

Let's examine seven common emotions and see how they reveal our self-centeredness, and then explore how each emotion can be used to draw us into a closer walk with God. In the process, we will see how our negative emotions can lead us to the source of our fulfillment.

ENVY—DESIRE FOR GAIN

Envy is the desire to gain what appears to make others happy—a bigger home, a better car, a higher paying job. We think that having these things will finally make us content.

Perhaps we keep our eyes upon Christ most of the day, knowing that He alone fulfills us, but in quiet moments early in the morning, during coffee break, on the drive to and from work, the green cloud of envy settles over us and we wish we had more of what the Joneses have. They appear to be so happy. But if we lived with them for a few weeks, we might discover they are just good actors. Behind their closed door, Mr. and Mrs. Jones may be wishing they had what we have.

I rarely experience envy any more. But for many years it often engulfed me, especially when I traveled with members of Dale's management team. The subject of money inevitably surfaced and we would compare salaries. I could tell that each of us was trying to understand why one person made more or less than another.

I never revealed my salary but I learned that one of my subordinates was making significantly more than I, even though he had far less experience in the business. For several days and nights I felt envy and anger because of that inequity. I formulated several plans to reveal the injustice without sounding like I was complaining. But Dale discovered the mistake about the same time I did and doubled my salary before I even had a chance to talk to him. It had been an innocent oversight. Dale had been so immersed in his cause that he rarely thought about the financial rewards to himself or others in the business. But doubling my salary did not eliminate my envy because there was always someone else in the company who made more money and had more things. I came to realize that money and possessions would never fill my cup. *The only good my envy served was as a reminder that God alone is my source of life.*

The reason I seldom feel envy any more is because I know that nothing others have can permanently satisfy. When I do feel envy, I pray, "Lord, thank You for this emotion. Help me see that what I want can never fill me up as much as You can. In fact, looking for happiness in Your creation is like idol worship in your eyes. I'm glad You honor those who turn from idols to worship You" (based on 1 Thessalonians 1:9).

The next emotion is closely related to envy.

JEALOUSY—FEAR OF LOSS

Whereas envy is wanting something we don't have, jealousy is the fear of losing what we already possess.

Jealousy is what we feel when someone flirts with our mate, when a special friend moves away, or when our position at work is threatened.

In high school, I dated Susan fairly steadily for nearly three years. During our senior year she went to California for a vacation and when she returned she informed me that she had met another guy. Those next few days I was miserably jealous. I lost ten pounds in two days. I couldn't concentrate on my after-school job, and my boss finally told me either to quit or to make up with my girlfriend.

After the boss's ultimatum, I left work early and went over to Susan's house. When I told her how miserable I was, she broke down and cried. What a thrill it was to have her back. But the excitement didn't last very long. Within a month, we were having major problems. I was constantly questioning the relationship. I was never sure she wouldn't leave me again. Instead of being able to relax and enjoy her company, my fear of losing her a second time drove away all my positive feelings and made me suspicious of any other guy who talked to her.

Although I didn't realize it at the time, I can see now that my jealousy actually revealed my own pride. I wanted control of the relationship and of her. If we were going to break up again, I wanted to be the one to do it, not her.

Negative emotions reveal to us that we are viewing the world as if its only purpose is to satisfy our needs. When we expect individuals and things to cooperate with our specially designed program to bring us satisfaction, it's not surprising that we get envious and jealous when those goals are frustrated, delayed, or postponed.

As with envy, to counteract jealousy I approach the Lord in prayer: "Lord, I'm afraid of losing something that I already have. However, I want my treasure to be in heaven, not here. I realize that whatever I have that I enjoy can never permanently fill my cup. Even if I lose something I need, I can come to You, the giver of life, and ask for another. And if You don't want me to have it, I can ask You to take away the desire. Thank You that You, not my possessions, are the source of life."

Some men fear losing their wife because it would end their best friendship as well as their sexual outlet. They fail to remember that God can handle every need. Andre Thornton, a major league baseball player whose wife was killed in a tragic car accident, understands this truth. Andre honestly faced his emotions through prayer:

> I asked God to quench my sex drive, even though since the accident I hadn't felt any sexual feelings whatsoever. But I knew myself well enough to know that someday those desires would return. I knew the temptations that came to professional athletes. I knew the women that hung around baseball teams. There would be opportunities on road trips to get into compromising situations, and I didn't want to do anything to disgrace the name of Christ. So I asked God to kill any sexual desires until He brought along someone to take Gert's place in my life. God was faithful in answering this prayer too.*

Some people have a hard time admitting that the warning light of jealousy is flashing in their life.

---

*Thornton, Andre, as told to Al Janssen, *Triumph Born of Tragedy* (Eugene, Ore.: Harvest House, 1983), 105.

But letting it flash too long can cause major problems. Spouses, children, and possessions are simply on loan to us from the Lord. We do not own them. Continually fearing the loss of a person or a possession can end in emotional and spiritual defeat.

The next emotion is probably one of the most destructive desires drawing men and women away from God. At almost every men's retreat I teach I am asked to address this subject. At conferences for pro athletes when we have a question-and-answer-time for men only, this topic always comes up first.

LUST—A FANTASYLAND DREAM

Lust makes us think that having some person we don't have would make us happier. Often that person is a figment of our imagination. Even if the person is real, we often attach character traits to him or her that are not real. Usually our lust focuses on sexual involvement. We imagine someone terribly fond of us who prefers our presence and intimacy over anyone else's. We imagine that if we had such a person to hold in our arms, it would be exciting and wonderfully fulfilling. This is a terrible deception, for we forget or ignore the devastating consequences of carrying out our imaginations.

Sensual imaginations reveal our selfish desire for stimulation. Unchecked, sensual stimulation actually increases the desire. We see this exhibited in several ways. For example, one of the primary reasons people smoke or consume alcohol or drugs is to stimulate their physical senses.

As a person continues in this selfish frame of mind, the desire grows until he needs regular and increasing doses of stimulation. That's one reason for the child pornography craze today. Men who stimulate their minds through sensual photographs need increasingly kinkier or more violent pictures to remain stimulated. The same is true with sexual involvement in marriage. If our primary motivation for sex is self-centered—to have our mate stimulate us—we tend to need more and more varied forms of sex to remain stimulated.

Even if we feel we've conquered lust, the emotion can strike when we least expect it. One friend discovered this when he spoke at a Christian conference. Dick's wife was in the final months of pregnancy, so they were not as sexually active as usual. While several hundred miles away from home, Dick suddenly found himself infatuated with a woman attending the conference. She was attractive and seemed to enjoy his company. But while admitting his normal sexual drive was heating up, he also knew that yielding to that desire would bring at best only a very temporary satisfaction. He came face to face with his own selfish desire to be stimulated and realized that the devastating long-term consequences to his ministry, to his wife and kids, and to his relationship with God would far outweigh any momentary pleasure. That knowledge helped him control his physical drive, which took about forty-eight hours to subside.

The motivation behind extramarital affairs seems to be very different for men and women. Men tend to lust for physical release or conquest, viewing women as challenges for satisfying their sexual drives. Women, on the other hand, tend to involve themselves in affairs because of their deep need for communication and a meaningful relationship that is not being met.

How can we use this emotion to strengthen our relationship with God? First, by recognizing the basic motive behind lust. Lust is not serving a person in love; it is viewing a person as an object to be used. This happens even in marriage. With Norma, I had to realize that I was violating God's law by trying to use her for my own happiness rather than loving her by serving her needs.

Second, lust can reconfirm our awareness that God—not another's body, not even our mate's—is the source of our fulfillment. As pleasurable as sex can be, it can never substitute for the lasting joy and satisfaction of knowing God.

Third, in the midst of lustful thoughts, as an act of our will, we can pray something like this: "Lord I know there are times when I wish my mate acted sexier. And there are even times I have thoughts about being in the arms of another person. All the advertisements on TV have tried to convince me it would be exciting. But right here and now I continue to trust You to fill my life with what I need. I am willing to rest and wait in Your faithfulness. I don't even know all I'm trying to gain from these lustful thoughts, but You know, and I know You'll meet my needs as You always have."

Since God knows our thoughts, we can share them with Him and admit we don't understand.

That's what Paul instructs us to do in Romans: "[God's] Spirit also helps our weakness; for we do not know how to pray as we should ... and He who searches the hearts knows what the mind of the Spirit is, because He intercedes for the saints according to the will of God" (Romans 8:26–27).

What practical help can we offer those stuck in the quicksand of lustful desire? Some try to struggle out of the grip it has on their lives through visualization, masturbation, or regular participation in sexual activity. But the more we struggle, the deeper we sink. If no one is available to pull us out, the one way to escape from quicksand is to relax, lie back in the sand, take a deep breath, fill your lungs with air, and allow your limbs to float to the top. We can take similar action with lust by not fighting our thoughts and desires and instead ask Jesus to perform what He promises to do—release us from bondage. He can supernaturally pull us out as we rest in Him.

Another way to escape from quicksand is to slowly move your arms above your head, sink them slightly into the sand, and swim slowly to the edge, as if doing a slow-motion backstroke. Experts say it may take several hours to swim just a few feet. But freedom is as close as the bank. We can do the same thing by persistently looking to Christ for strength and patience.

I have known men stuck in the mire of lust who didn't make it to freedom for several months. It may take a year for some to "swim" to freedom. Day after day we must reconfirm truths given to us by Christ. God promises He is faithful to answer the requests of His children. "Therefore I tell you, whatever you ask for in prayer, believe you have received it, and it will be yours" (Mark 11:24 NIV). And, "If you remain in me and my words remain in you, ask whatever you wish, and it will be given you" (John 15:7 NIV). Real freedom comes from abiding in a close relationship with God and from allowing God's Word to become alive in us. He says in His Word to live a life of love: "But among you there must not be even a *hint* of sexual immorality" (Ephesians 5:3 NIV). And "It is for freedom that Christ has set us free. Stand firm, then, and do not let yourselves be burdened again by a yoke of slavery" (Galatians 5:1 NIV). It is God's will that we experience freedom from lust, so we can stand in His line daily, knowing it is just a matter of time before He will bring us freedom from sexual slavery.

Once we're free from the quicksand, we're usually weak from the effort. Here are four ways to regain strength and remain strong to keep from falling back into the mire.

First, rehearse the negative consequences of sexual involvement, even in the midst of lustful thoughts. Remember what it feels like to be trapped. The consequences are far more than we can mention here, but they include enslavement to passion (Galatians 5:1), reinforcement of our self-centered tendency that diminishes genuine love, callousness of our soul (Ephesians 4:19), and, of course, the possibility of catching a sexual disease. In other words, the truth and life of God is darkened within us when we engage in unrighteousness (see Romans 1:18–32).

Second, memorize sections of Scripture that

deal specifically with sexual freedom. After memorizing them, persistently ask God to make your life consistent with those verses. Start with Galatians 5:1–14, Ephesians 5:1–6, and 1 Thessalonians 4:3–7.

Third, for men especially, beware of the anger/lust cycle that often develops. Many men experience their most severe times of lust after a struggle or problem at home or at work. If we fail to make things right after a disagreement or confrontation, we may be setting ourselves up for temptation because such encounters leave us feeling depressed and inadequate. Since none of us likes to feel badly about ourselves, we look for something to perk us up, to make us feel powerful and important again.

Sexual stimulation can have a temporary euphoric effect. Like alcohol or drugs, it can bring about a heightened sense of self-worth—until the shame and reality of our actions bring us crashing down. Some men who never take a drink or try drugs, submit to a life of erotic escapades that is every bit as addictive, and every bit as deadly.

Proverbs has sobering words for those who use any form of lust—actual sexual encounters, fantasy, or pornographic pictures—to make up for feelings of anger or low self-worth. "The lips of an adulteress drip honey, and her speech is smoother than oil; but in the end she is bitter as gall, sharp as a double-edged sword" (5:3–4 NIV).

Giving in to lust does not break the anger/lust cycle; it only intensifies it. Now we are not only angry and depressed about our problem at work or at home, but we are also angry about our lack of self-control. And on top of our shame, those of us who are Christians also have the Holy Spirit convicting us of sin.

Genuine repentance is a biblical solution, but getting furious with ourselves and vowing it will never happen again does little good. In fact, when we browbeat ourselves (a way of punishing ourselves so that God won't, or so that He will "let us off the hook") we actually dig a deeper rut for ourselves and set ourselves up for our next "lust fix."

Unless we truthfully deal with the anger/lust cycle and admit that it is signaling that a relationship needs repair or that we need the help of a Christian friend or counselor, we may continue in the downward spiral for years. This vicious circle of sin can cause even Christians to spin so fast that right seems wrong and wrong seems right.

Finally, realize that for most people gaining freedom from lust is a long-term process, especially for those who have developed a habit of immoral thoughts and actions. You might consider starting or joining a support group for those who struggle in this area. This can be a group of men or women (not in the same group) who testify as to how God has produced freedom and who encourage and support one another in memorizing and meditating on Scripture. They also hold each other accountable, pray with each other, and talk honestly about their entrapment. Much healing can come just by confessing our weakness and praying for each other: "Therefore, confess your sins to one another, and pray for one another, so that you may be healed. The effective prayer of a righteous man can accomplish much" (James 5:16).

Al meets regularly with several other men in a discipleship group. Once he returned from a business trip and reported that his hotel room had a cable movie station. He watched a PG-rated movie, then started to watch a sexually explicit film but caught himself and turned it off. However, he expressed concern about handling temptation on an upcoming ten-day trip. One of the members asked Al to develop a plan to use his time, which he did.

On his return Al had to give a report. He told how near the end of the trip he found himself seated next to a single woman at an athletic event. The thought entered his mind, "You could take her out for dinner and no one would ever know." Rather than allow time to entertain the thought any further, he left the game early. *Knowing he was accountable to men back home helped him resist temptation* because he knew they would ask him how he did.

I have focused on the sexual aspects of lust because it is so out of control in our society. But other forms—such as craving sweets, overeating, and stimulating the senses through drugs and alcohol—can be just as damaging. The thoughts I've shared can apply in any area of sensual temptation that robs us of life.

What warning lights flash most frequently in your life? Jealousy, envy, or lust? Take the time necessary to deal with those emotions.

6

Overcoming a Major Destroyer of Joy

HAVE YOU EVER walked confidently out on a long limb only to look back and see someone sawing it from the tree? That's how I felt at a church council meeting years ago. But the hurt I experienced that night led to one of the most important discoveries of my life. A discovery that not only drew me closer to Christ, but closer to the very people who hurt me as well.

Ordinarily church council meetings were un-eventful. Routine reports, budget reviews, and voting usually sent everyone home yawning. Confident that I had performed an above-average job for my second year out of seminary, I delivered my report enthusias-tically, hoping to add some excitement to the typi-cally boring meeting. The excitement I generated, however, was not the kind I expected. My recommen-dations concerned what I considered obvious needs, particularly the purchase of a church bus for the youth. I assumed I had the support of the pastor and the Sunday school committee before this meeting. But instead of endorsing my recommendations and expressing what a wonderful job I had done as assistant pastor, each council member started criticizing me. Why didn't I run the youth group as it had been run in previous years? I should slow down in making so many changes. Did I think my ways were superior? They'd been doing things the same way for fifteen years. Why were they suddenly wrong when I came? They were especially critical of the bus because of the complications and negative elements it would bring to the youth group. Plus the cost would be prohibitive.

HURT FEELINGS—NO ONE APPRECIATES MY GOALS

The sudden and intense criticism stunned me, and I was offended that no one on my committee supported me, not even the pastor. I thought to myself, "They don't pay me enough to take this kind of abuse. Why am I subjecting myself to this? Somewhere there must be a church where people would appreciate my talents. It's obvious this congregation doesn't want me."

I slithered home that night and woke Norma to pour out my woes. I complained about how I'd been mistreated and suggested that I ought to quit. She tried to encourage me.

Unable to sleep, I sat in the kitchen and pondered my situation. I reached for my Bible but didn't feel like reading it. On the scratch pad by the phone I wrote, "Why do people in the church continue to hurt my feelings? Why do they make me so angry?" "Lord," I pleaded, "show me what I can do for these poor people. How can I penetrate the hardness of their hearts? What would it take to break through their stubborn resistance and help them see Your love?" If necessary, I was willing to stay up all night and read every chapter of the Bible to find help. I was tired of having my emotions manipulated by members of the church.

For several hours, I could not figure out what to do to help those people. It never occurred to me that my conflict with the church might be my fault, that I might need to change or adjust some attitudes and actions. I could only think that if they were more supportive, more committed to Christ, more dedicated, then I'd be happy. If they'd only step out of the past and start implementing my fresh ideas, I wouldn't have these problems.

Sound familiar? No wonder Jesus said in Matthew 7:3: "And why do you look at the speck that is in your brother's eye, but do not notice the log that is in your own eye?"

Sometime early the next morning, light began to dawn in my mind and I caught a glimpse of the log in my own eye: I wasn't *serving* these people; I had unconsciously tried to *use* them for my own self-centered goals. I had learned many creative ways to run a church education program in seminary. Implementing those ideas became my goal for this church. Though I never verbalized it, I expected the pastor, the Sunday school committee, and the church membership to follow me without question. Couldn't they recognize the genius of my fresh, creative ideas? I interpreted their negative response to my many new ideas as a personal rejection of me.

When church members did not cooperate with my personal goals I got hurt feelings. But how could they possibly cooperate if they didn't know my goals? I had never shared them—that would have exposed my self-centeredness. I had forgotten what a genuine minister is—one who *serves* the needs of those around him. No wonder the church reacted against me. I had never bothered to find out *their* goals. I hurt their feelings because I changed their programs, and they hurt my feelings because they did not cooperate with my unstated goals.

UNDERSTANDING AND USING HURT FEELINGS

Hurt feelings are closely connected with anger but are slightly different. Unchecked, they can lead to anger, then bitterness, and even depression. Hurt feelings are those frustrating emotions that emerge from the unexpected. They let us know we are trying to use someone for our own benefit who is not cooperating with us.

Usually when our feelings are hurt it's because we had hoped that the offending individual would make us happy in some way. We may have expected the person to say or do something that we planned to use for our own fulfillment. When the person didn't cooperate, we may have responded with tears, pouting, an angry reaction, or quiet disappointment, hoping that our reaction might provoke the person to change and treat us in the way we first expected. If the person refused to change, we may have tried the silent treatment for two or three days. We may have been tempted to get even or to run to someone else for sympathy.

ESCAPING THE PAIN OF HURT FEELINGS

That night after my disastrous church council meeting, the first thing I had to do was *admit* my problem. With deep conviction I confessed: "Lord, I never realized until now the fuller meaning of what a real servant is." Somehow I had forgotten that the second most important commandment He gave us is to love one another. I had misrepresented myself as a minister, especially as an assistant pastor. To my shame, I hadn't even taken the time to ask the one I was assisting what direction he wanted to go. Where did the pastor want to take the church? What did he feel was important? What would he like me to do? My primary objective had been to design my own program and to find ways to get everyone, including the pastor, to follow it. Did I only want a successful program that would reflect my talent and lead me to bigger and better positions?

I never did get to sleep that night, and I could hardly wait to get to church in the morning. When I arrived I immediately called the pastor to ask if I could see him. When he invited me into his office, I confessed, "Pastor, that board meeting was rough last night. But it showed me something very important.

Early this morning I realized that I have been violating a major biblical principle. For two years I have tried to get everyone in this church to follow my program, my goals, my vision. It's honestly never occurred to me, as your assistant, to ask you where God is leading you to take this church."

"After the meeting last night, I thought the reason you wanted to see me was to resign," he said with a smile.

I asked him to forgive me for my poor example as a minister and as his assistant. Then I asked him to share with me his goals and how I might assist him in reaching them. I wanted to learn how to use all my resources and training to help him, the church council, the youth sponsors, and the members of the church to reach their own spiritual goals.

That was the turning point in our relationship. He not only forgave me, but he immediately started treating me like a son. He still got frustrated with me occasionally, but instead of allowing my feelings to be hurt I would ask what I could do to help remove any roadblocks from his ministry or how I could be an encouragement or comfort to him.

That incident was not the only time I have seen the depth of my self-centeredness. There have been other humbling moments when my feelings have been hurt, even by my loving wife, Norma.

Last summer Norma and I attended a dinner party. During a discussion about the quality of life in Phoenix, I proudly announced that it's like paradise. In the winter you can have a fire in your fireplace almost every night and still swim in an outdoor pool during the day.

When someone asked how cold it actually gets in the winter, I quipped, "It can drop into the low 20s."

Norma laughed and said, "That shows how observant he is," and went right on talking.

I didn't hear anything else she said. My feelings were hurt. I couldn't understand why she would make such a belittling statement and embarrass me in front of all those people. Besides, I was sure I knew how cold it gets in Phoenix. I was tempted to ask the hosts if they had an encyclopedia. I wanted to prove I wasn't stupid.

It bothered me so much that I didn't speak to Norma on the way home. When she asked if anything was wrong, I snapped, "No!" I had a cauldron full of emotions churning within. I was ashamed for feeling so hurt, yet angry that she would be so insensitive. When I finally mentioned the problem, she apologized and said she hadn't meant the statement to come out that way. Yet I remembered her words and still felt irritated.

Before I fell asleep, I prayed, "Lord, as hard as it is to express these words, thank You that my feelings were hurt tonight. This 'red light' helps me see again my own self-centered tendencies. What those people think of me does not matter because their opinions have nothing to do with my self-worth. Only Your opinion matters. Norma didn't mean to hurt my feelings, and my reaction to her comments reveals that I have filled my cup with something that doesn't belong in it—other people's opinions. I expected Norma to say things to make me look intelligent. I guess that shows how quickly we can drift from You. Before I fall asleep, I want to thank You that I can look to You for my fulfillment rather than to Norma or anyone else." My hurt lasted only a few more minutes and was gone by the time I drifted off to sleep.

Even when someone deliberately tries to hurt our feelings we can still apply this principle. We don't have to allow hurt feelings to defeat us.

ANGER—SOMEONE OR SOMETHING IS BLOCKING MY GOAL

Anger is a very close relative of hurt feelings. As another important warning light, it usually indicates that our focus has shifted so that we are expecting fulfillment from God's creation rather than from God Himself.

Anger can erupt at any moment, and it's not always directed at a person. Sometimes we get angry at circumstances, such as a construction detour. The anger we express is evidence that we expect our environment to cooperate and meet our needs. As mentioned in an earlier chapter, we expect the "four P's" to add something to our fullness. We're frustrated because we believe we're about to lose something we thought was secure. Or we realize we may not gain something we expected.

Before a woman marries, she often has clear expectations concerning her future husband. He will communicate all his goals, expectations, and feelings; he will comfort and hold her when she needs him; he will make her feel special.

After three or four years of marriage, however, some of these women conclude that it would have been less painful to remain single. Their blocked expectations are often reflected in anger and expressed in explosive outbursts or nagging irritation. Other women may hold their anger inside so that only their pastors or psychiatrists know for sure. They are the ones who will see the damage caused by repressed anger.

The same thing is true for men—wives and children may frustrate their personal expectations and eat holes in their emotional cup.

One father we know has been furious with his son for three years because he married a girl from a different social class. What the father won't admit is that his anger is actually a reflection of his own self-centered expectations.

When people and things frustrate our personal goals, anger results. My anger level has dropped significantly over the last several years as I've realized that no person or thing can take away what God has given me. If I lose something of material worth, I know God can replace it if I really need it. So I can relax without feeling compelled to manipulate my circumstances.

I'm not completely free from anger, however. I still tend to use people for my own advantage by setting secret goals for them. When they don't cooperate, I become frustrated and angry. This happened when my family agreed we should write a parenting book. Our goal for the book was that it would help parents stay in harmony with their

children, build their children's self-worth, motivate
them to be courteous, and to help them attain their
God-given potential.

What happened on those days when my
children were disrespectful or unmotivated or out of
harmony—in other words, when they were normal
children and we were normal parents? I became
angry because they blocked my goal of helping
thousands of families through our book. I was afraid
that my goal would go down the drain if anyone got
wind that things weren't perfect in the Smalley home.
So I lectured my children—until I stopped and
thought about what I was doing. Then I realized I was
standing in the wrong line again, expecting
fulfillment from the people reading this book rather
than from God.

We have a saying in our house, "Am I making
you angry or am I revealing your self-centeredness?"
With three honest children and a very honest wife, I
must often admit that my own self-centeredness is at
the bottom of a problem or disagreement.

People do not really make us angry.

We may think people make us angry, but most
of the time they simply reveal our own selfishness.
What usually makes us angry is our lack of control
over people and circumstances.

If I get angry at someone who insults me and
deliberately tries to make me angry, I am making a

personal decision. He cannot *make* me angry. Unless I have been secretly trying to convince him how wonderful I am, there is no reason for me to be upset at his accusation. So once again, anger reveals self-centeredness. I am angry because someone does not think of me the way I want him to think.

Under similar circumstances, parents often become angry at their children. If a child does something to embarrass a parent in front of the parent's adult friends, the parent often becomes angry, because adults (just like teens) want their friends to think well of them. The fear of losing social status or approval has spurred many angry reactions.

One of the most difficult lessons for many of us to learn is to stop trying to gain the approval of others. Expecting to find our true self-image reflected in the opinion of others is like going into a house of mirrors to find out what we really look like. Each person, like each mirror, will tell us something different. One person may admire us for being "open-minded," but someone else may criticize us for "having no convictions." One person may tell us our new outfit is "divine," but someone else might comment, "I had no idea they made outfits like that in your size."

To deal with anger we must come to grips with the fact that we are not all-powerful. Until we can see people and circumstances through the eyes of a sovereign God, we will never be free from trying to control what others do to us and think about us.

Yet all anger is not directed toward others. Many times anger is disgust at our own ineptitude.

After speaking to a group of more than four hundred men recently, I berated myself on the drive home. "Smalley, how could you give such a lousy talk? Why in the world did you use that stupid illustration? No one laughed, and it didn't even fit in your outline. They must think you're a real jerk. There goes your reputation!"

In the middle of my mental tirade, I recognized what I was doing and shifted into a prayer: "Lord, thank You that I'm angry and disgusted with myself. Being accepted by those men has nothing to do with my fulfillment. I thank You for loving me and filling me and being so faithful to me for so many years. I want to improve my speaking skills, Lord, and I plan to do that. But I know those skills have nothing to do with You and me."

Then I put some Christian music in my tape deck and sang praise songs the rest of the way home. It took about ten minutes for the anger to subside and for me to feel free, ready to continue with life. I could have spent days feeling like a failure, but instead I used the opportunity to learn more about myself and God.

As we examine the remaining emotions, we may discover we are all more self-centered than we thought. Although recognizing our self-centeredness is never pleasant, unless we honestly admit our selfish motives we cannot begin to use our negative emotions for positive gain.

RIGHTEOUS ANGER—IS THERE SUCH A THING?

"Loving anger" is a legitimate form of this usually negative emotion, but I rarely see it in myself or others. Righteous anger is spawned by injustice to another and motivates us to help, not harm, both the victim and the offender. For instance, if someone you know is robbed and beaten, righteous anger would grieve with the victim and gently guide that person to emotional health. It would also grieve over the sickness of the attacker and, if possible, firmly and directly love that person to wholeness.

Although there are times to be righteously indignant, those who are honest must admit that most of our anger is the result of self-centeredness. If we are willing, however, we can learn to use this anger to strengthen our relationship with God.

USING ANGER IN A POSITIVE WAY

First, we need to thank God for the flashing light that shows us the connection between our anger and our selfishness. Thanksgiving is an expression of trust and obedience. It's a way of saying we want to follow His way rather than our own.

Second, we need to determine why we're angry. Blocked goals are the most common cause of anger, and anger over blocked goals reveals our selfish nature.

Third, we need to admit our self-centeredness. The promise of 1 John 1:9–10 is that if we *confess* our sin (of selfishness), God is faithful to forgive us and to cleanse us. If we think we're not sinners—if we rationalize our anger and insist that we're not being selfish—we lie and the truth is not in us.

We may feel that admitting our selfish ways

degrades us, but being aware of natural tendencies has nothing to do with personal worth. Some people think confessing means they must constantly chant the refrain "Such a worm as I." That is not God's message! However, if we desire a close, dependent relationship with Christ, we must admit daily, and sometimes hourly, that we are tempted to use an aspect of God's creation to fill our cup. Sometimes we may even surrender to that temptation and become angry when the created thing doesn't fulfill our expectations.

Anger imprisons some people. Those who are violent or verbally abusive in their anger, or who are overly critical of themselves and others probably will need more help than I can offer in a few pages. Never hesitate to ask for help from qualified Christian counselors and pastors, however. Your willingness to face the problem and deal with it is a sign of strength. Also, a number of excellent books can help you further understand why people continue in their anger and how you can break the vicious cycle. I've listed some of them at the end of this book.

Fourth, we need to pray a simple but meaningful prayer expressing to God that we realize He is the source of life. Here are some examples:

- "Lord, whether or not I make it to my appointment on time has nothing to do with my fulfillment."

- "Lord, the fact that Norma bought white bread rather than whole wheat does not mean I cannot have a fulfilling life."

- "Lord, having to take the time to remove Mike's bike from the driveway cannot rob me of Your joy."

- "Lord, buying the wrong part for this repair job means I'll lose a few minutes, but that won't drain my cup. So what if I have to drive back to the store? It won't mean a thing in a year."

For many people, it is the little inconveniences like those listed above that bring on an angry response. But anger can also be a response to much more serious issues.

Over the past several years we have seen many people with deep emotional struggles resulting from tragic circumstances: a woman whose husband had abandoned her and their four school-age children; a man who had given all his savings (including his retirement fund money) to a "Christian" builder who left town with the money and left behind thousands of dollars of debts; a young woman who waited with a chapel full of guests for a groom who never showed up; and a corporate manager who worked for years to reach the top, only to have his company bought out in a hostile takeover, leaving him jobless at age 61.

Possessions, position, places, and people. The loss of these caused severe hurt and anger for each of these people. But when they discovered the source of lasting life and recognized their anger as a flashing light warning them that they were operating without the power of a sovereign God who could more than compensate for their loss, they were able to deal with their loss instead of letting it devastate them.

We helped each one through weeks of necessary grief. Then, when they were ready, we walked with them into a personal, healing relationship with Christ.

Martin Luther once said about temptation, "You cannot keep birds from flying over your head, but you can keep them from building a nest in your hair." The same is true with anger. We cannot control the circumstances that make us angry, but we can control how we respond to them. We can resist the temptation to let our circumstances make us angry.

Let's switch gears now and discuss an area that's brought to us by the producers of upset stomachs. This section combines the two emotions that keep many of us up late at night and can hinder all our relationships, especially our relationship with God. We can look at them together.

FEAR AND WORRY—WHAT IF I CAN'T ACHIEVE MY GOALS

How many of us pass through a day without experiencing one or both of these emotions? Fretting about the implications of some action or dreading what may happen in the future is common, but not healthy. All of us are familiar with that gnawing, sickening feeling that eats at our insides when the promotion we expected and needed to meet financial obligations is in jeopardy; when something we treasure is in danger of being lost; when we are given an ultimatum—accept a transfer to a strange city or look for another job; or when a person we respect has lost confidence in us.

Fear reveals our attitude toward personal loss. The greater the loss, the greater the fear. Worry, a form of fear, is preoccupation with the possibility that we may lose something valuable.

One weekend my lawyer told me I needed to call him first thing Monday morning because he had received correspondence from the Internal Revenue Service. For hours over the next two days I worried, imagining all kinds of horrible scenarios—getting audited, owing thousands of dollars, learning I wasn't doing what I should be doing, getting a lien slapped on my house. On and on the thoughts persisted.

To make matters worse, I couldn't reach him on Monday! When I finally talked to him Tuesday afternoon, I learned that he couldn't make a corporate decision about my company without knowing if I intended to change the name of the company. It was a minor question, certainly not worth spending any time worrying about. That same day I received a letter from him saying he had thoroughly checked out our finances with my accountant and everything was in order. How typical. We often waste valuable energy worrying about something that turns out to be insignificant.

REASONS FOR FEAR AND WORRY

Whenever I begin to feel fear or worry I thank the Lord for the feeling, then test the following six reasons until I understand the source. Simply identifying the reason for my worry often calms my anxiety. I remember these six areas by trying to pronounce a word spelled FRMPTH (sounds like *from the*).

Future—Am I worried about something in my future? For a young single person, it might be college or a future mate or a possible job. Some might worry about earning enough money to provide for a family. Someone who's sick might be anxious about achieving long-term goals. Whatever it is, recognize that it cannot give permanent fulfillment.

Reputation—Am I worried that my reputation will be smeared? Sometimes I fear being on television because I'm afraid I will say something to embarrass myself or my family or God. If that's the basis for my worry, I take the simple steps we'll discuss in the next chapter and the anxiety disappears almost immediately.

Money—Am I worried about losing money or not gaining enough money? I remind myself that money does not provide fulfillment. Like Paul, God can bring me to the place where I am content whether I have much or little (Philippians 4:10–18).

Possessions—Am I worried about losing or not gaining possessions? I identify the items and then remember Jim Elliot's statement: "He is no fool who gives up what he cannot keep to gain what he cannot lose."

Time—Am I worried about not having enough time? I ask myself the following questions: Is someone misusing my time? (If we don't set our own schedules, someone else is likely to do it for us.) Am I procrastinating? Am I up against an impossible writing deadline? I remind myself that God controls time and that He has given me enough to accomplish all He wants me to do. So I resolve to use it wisely and to respond to each interruption as if it came from God. Even if worry about unmet deadlines awakens me in the middle of the night I need not worry about not getting enough sleep. Instead I can use the time for fellowship with God, which in itself is gain. With the Lord, tomorrow's loss or gain cannot affect my fulfillment. So I can relax and even enjoy my insomnia. Usually that helps me fall asleep.

Health—Am I worried about losing my health or getting old? Do I get discouraged when I find more wrinkles and gray hairs? Do I worry about my weight? On these occasions I remind myself that my health is in God's hands and that even poor health cannot keep me from having a fulfilling life. When I was in seminary I worried about my reputation, which caused my stomach to churn, which made me worry about getting an ulcer, which made me worry that people would discover I was not at peace with God, which would ruin my reputation! Of all people, how could a minister not be at peace with God? Now, however, I know that having people think well of me offers only temporary satisfaction at best, but I still need to remind myself often of the futility of trying to convince others of my spiritual value.

One way to counteract fear and worry associated with any of the above causes is to recall memorized Scripture. For example, meditating on portions of Psalm 37, 62, or 103 helps put problems in perspective. Think on the meaning of phrases such as "Do not fret because of evildoers," "Delight yourself in the Lord," "Better is the little of the righteous than the abundance of many wicked," "The steps of a man are established by the Lord . . . when he falls, he shall not be hurled headlong; because the Lord is the One who holds his hand," "[The Lord] is my rock and my salvation, my stronghold; I shall not be greatly shaken," and "God is a refuge for us."

A friend of mine who is a prolific writer used to spend weeks worrying when he sent a proposal to a publisher, wondering how it would be received. Rejection notices devastated him. He worried about what he was doing wrong and what it would take to be published. Rather than motivating him to resubmit his work or to improve his craft, rejection immobilized him, making him unable to write at all for days.

My friend no longer suffers from fear and worry, however. Recently he told me about submitting an article idea to a national magazine in which he really wants to be published. The rejection letter disappointed him, but instead of giving in to depression, he took a short walk and prayed, "Lord, thank You for this rejection. I know that being published in this magazine would be a real achievement, but I also know that it won't give me lasting fulfillment. Lord, I only want to be published where You want me to be. Allow me to be free from anxiety and to continue to do the work You've called me to do. Whether I'm ever published in this magazine or not, I thank You that we're always together. You, Lord, are what brings me life." Within thirty minutes he was back at his desk, working hard on another book, with no feelings of worry to inhibit him.

What makes negative emotions like worry and fear exciting is that we can deal with them as warning lights and move on with productive lives. They don't have to defeat us when we understand Who they point us to.

LONELINESS—NO ONE SHARES MY GOAL

From the moment of birth we need other people. In fact, newborn babies are more helpless than almost any other creature. Yet our need for relationships is a double-edged sword. The fulfillment we find in relationships is sharply contrasted by feelings of emptiness when we are alone.

God Himself is a God of relationships. In the beginning, God said, "Let *us* make man in *our* image (Genesis 1). The Father, Son, and Spirit mirror our need to be in relationship to others and explain the emptiness and frustration we feel when we are alone.

Perhaps one reason the Lord provided us with a "family of believers" is so we would always have spiritual mothers, fathers, sisters, and brothers to love us (see 1 Timothy 5). A loving church can be a haven for lonely people.

Yet for some people, the loneliness they feel is not based on a lack of people in their lives, but on their own selfish actions or desires. Jim's wife, Betty, had just delivered their second child in less than two years. With all the demands on Betty's time, Jim began to feel left out and unwanted. He turned to a secretary at work to boost his self-worth, and in almost no time they were having an affair.

Jim set out to end his feelings of loneliness in a sinful way, and he only compounded his pain. Today, four years later, his wife and children live in another state and the other woman is living with another man. For Jim, the pain keeps driving his loneliness deeper and deeper—and may for years to come.

Although Jim's example is extreme, loneliness can be a symptom of a selfish desire to control another's time or affection—even if it is not best for them or others.

When the birth of Michael, our third child, required me to stop traveling as much, I often shuttled the travel team back and forth from the office to the airport. After dropping them off I'd feel lonely whenever I recalled their parting statements: "We'll miss you in Minneapolis"; "We'll say 'hi' to all your friends in Seattle"; or "We'll bring you some bread from San Francisco." I'd drive back to an empty office, sometimes feeling resentment toward Michael for what he had denied me. I had to learn that only Christ, not those trips nor even the camaraderie, could give me lasting fulfillment. The loneliness I felt was selfish, not genuine. Once I learned that truth I was free to stay home, where I found out how much more rewarding it was to have extra time with my wife and kids. Since then, I've thanked Michael time and time again for helping me learn this truth.

Like all the other negative emotions we discussed, loneliness can draw us closer to God. How? First, we need to know why we are lonely. Most often we are wishing we had someone near us to share our life experiences. We want someone to return to us the same level of affection we wish to give. Although the desire for companionship is natural and good, expecting others to meet all our needs can lead to frustration. Even "best friends" and spouses have limits to the amount of time they can spend with us.

Second, while we're feeling lonely, we need to recognize that we are treating God the same way we feel life is treating us. Just as we want someone in God's creation to return our affection, God wants us to return to Him the affection He pours out on us. Lonely days and cold winter evenings can depress us. But they also give us time to hear God's gentle voice—if we listen closely—which calls us to look into the eyes of the One who said, "I will never desert you, nor will I ever forsake you" (Hebrews 13:5).

Third, we need to return our mind and spirit to the Lord by praying something like this: "Lord, I know that You want all of my heart and soul and mind focused on You as the source of my life. I keep forgetting this and I continually try to make Your creation fill my cup. But at this very moment I look to You as my only God. You are my source of lasting life. Lord, You know how I desire to share my life with someone, either a good friend or a mate. I ask You to bring that person into my life, but I'm willing to wait however long is necessary to have Your best. And I only want to see this person as overflow, because I want You to continue to be my very best friend. In the meantime show me how to enrich my relationship with You and with those around me."

For some, loneliness may last longer than expected. Our prayer needs to persist as long as loneliness lasts. If it doesn't disappear quickly we may be tempted to rely on tranquilizers or other artificial means to counteract it, but depending on an aspect of creation will only allow loneliness to entrench itself more deeply. On the other hand, the more we recognize Christ as the source of life and the more we see His faithfulness, the sooner joy and peace will replace loneliness. Plus, reaching out to others increases our joy. One of the best ways to find meaningful friendships is to be the kind of friend to others that *we* would like to have.

This is not an exhaustive list of negative emotions. We could examine many others, but the principles for achieving victory are all very similar.

Knowing how to use natural negative emotions to strengthen our relationship with God has tremendous value, but think how great it would be if we could also use everyday trials, both small and great, to pull us closer to God. The next chapter uncovers one of the most exciting truths I have learned: how trials, hardships, and difficulties can be the doorway to a richer life, how they can lead us to live in God's will. Believe it or not, trials can make us more loving. And perhaps best of all, trials can even increase our sense of personal worth. Talk about an overflowing life—this is it!

7

Letting Trials Produce
Love and Self-worth

MONTE JOHNSON, an eight-year veteran with the Oakland Raiders' professional football team, faced the most devastating crisis of his life. Would he be cut off from the team? Would he be traded? He had five months to worry.

Monte never started a game as an undergraduate at the University of Nebraska, but he attracted the attention of pro scouts in an all-star game, and Oakland drafted him. He went on to become a starting linebacker and played for the Super Bowl champions in 1977. Then tragedy struck. In a pre-season game against the Washington Redskins, a teammate accidentally hit him on a kickoff return, destroying the ligaments and cartilage in Monte's knee. While his teammates went on to win the Super Bowl again that year, Monte worked diligently to rehabilitate his knee. But when I saw him the next year, he told me there was a real possibility he would never play football again. Training camp was five months away, but already his anxiety over the situation was straining all his relationships.

"I have no idea what I want to do after football," he told me. "I had planned to play at least two more years. Even my wife doesn't understand that my career may be over."

What good can possibly come from an injured knee? Or from flunking third grade? Or from losing several thousand dollars in a business deal? Or from being an abused child? Or from any other tragic circumstance? Although each of these situations was initially devastating to the victim, each eventually produced "gold" in the afflicted person.

Many of us have been tricked into believing the world's viewpoint that suffering is bad and to be avoided whenever possible. But the words of the apostle Paul say otherwise: "God causes all things to work together for good ..." (Romans 8:28). How can any good be found in an illness or child abuse? Intellectually we believe the scriptural promise that *all things* work together for good, but most of us have wondered at one time or another what the *good* could possibly be.

I am convinced that the promise of Romans 8:28 is true in *every* case. In all my years of counseling and study, I have never found an exception, but it took me a long time to discover how to *find* the good in each trial. The concepts in this chapter have transformed my life and the lives of many others. I compare life to a treasure hunt because I know that in every negative situation God buries a valuable treasure that He wants us to have. Sometimes we have to search diligently for it. But if we search, we can find it.

I'm not implying that God causes all trials. I do not believe God was responsible for Judy's rape or for Jill's repeated sexual abuse by her uncle and brothers. Nor do I believe that God caused David's wife to take their children and desert him or that He caused Denise's parents to verbally and emotionally assault her. Judy, Jill, David, and Denise suffered years of emotional trauma from these trials until they learned how to treasure hunt. Buried in the debris of their tragedies were benefits as real as rubies and diamonds. As they dug into their tribulations and discovered the gems, their self-worth soared. They once considered themselves worthless; but when they learned the process of turning negatives into positives they saw the great value they possessed. It worked for Monte Johnson too.

I asked Monte to turn his injured knee and possible release from the Raiders into a benefit. First, we examined his options. One was to play football again for the Raiders. Another was to be traded to another team. The third was to retire and go into another line of work. I asked Monte to write down the benefits of all three possibilities. The first one was easy—playing for the Raiders—but it took a while for Monte to see the benefits of the other two options.

I saw Monte again a year later and he couldn't wait to tell me his experience. He had taken time to write down all the benefits he could think of for the two negative options—being traded or retiring from pro football. In both possibilities he saw ways to grow spiritually and to minister to other hurting people. He began getting ideas for developing a business. If he retired, he would have more time for his family. When he arrived at training camp, he was excited because he knew that whatever happened would be for his good. He saw an almost equal number of benefits in all three options.

At summer camp, after a thorough physical exam, the coach told Monte the bad news. His knee was not strong enough to handle the rigors of football; he would have to retire. The first words out of Monte's mouth shocked the coach. "I want to thank God for choosing you to be the instrument to help me discover what God wants me to do," Monte said. "Thank you for eight great years with the Raider organization."

Flabbergasted at such an unusual reaction from a player who had just been cut, the coach could think of nothing more to say. Monte gave him a hug and thanked him again for his years with the team.

Professional athletes dread retirement. Being told that their career is over at an age when most men are entering the prime of life devastates many of them. What made the difference for Monte was the time he'd spent treasure hunting. He uncovered the benefits and learned to see the experience as an opportunity rather than as a trial.

Several months after his release from the Raiders, Monte became involved in a financial counseling and management program to help athletes and other professionals plan for the future—a ministry that has helped hundreds of people.

Anyone can do what Monte did.

Every problem—great or small—has in it a treasure waiting to be discovered. The secret to successful treasure hunting is understanding two life-changing words: faith and love.

FAITH

Christ's teaching on faith will show us its true meaning if we pay attention to how He helped distraught people through their trials. In one situation Jesus praised a Roman soldier for having "great faith." A few hours later, Jesus rebuked His disciples for exercising "little faith." Let's see if we can determine the difference.

GREAT FAITH VS. LITTLE FAITH

In Matthew 8 a Roman officer came to Jesus and said, "Sir, my servant is lying paralyzed at home, suffering great pain." Even though the man made only a statement, not a request, Jesus answered, "'I will come and heal him.' But the centurion answered and said, 'Lord, I am not worthy for You to come under my roof, but just say the word, and my servant will be healed.'" Amazed by the centurion's faith, Christ said to the people around Him, "I have not found such *great faith* with anyone in Israel."

What prompted this response? In such a

religious country how could there be so little faith? What about the Pharisees and religious leaders? No doubt they were irritated by Christ's words and proud of the actions that demonstrated their faith. And what about the disciples? Surely they had faith.

What the soldier said that so impressed Christ was "Lord, I am not worthy for You to come under my roof, but *just say the word*, and my servant will be healed. For I, too, am a man *under authority*, with soldiers under me; and I say to this one, 'Go!' and he goes, and to another, 'Come!' and he comes, and to my slave, 'Do this!' and he does it."

The reason Jesus called the centurion's faith great was because the man believed without question that Jesus could heal his servant. He could picture in his mind how Jesus could order the deed done in the same way he ordered his soldiers or slaves. Jesus was under the Father's authority just as the centurion was under the authority of the Roman government. People obeyed the centurion because the empire delegated power to him just as the God of the universe delegated power to Jesus. Jesus fulfilled the man's expectation "as you have believed," and his servant was healed that very hour.

The story of the centurion stands in stark contrast to a later event that illustrated the weak faith of the disciples. Jesus told them to get into their boat and to cross to the other side of the lake. Undoubtedly exhausted from an intense day of ministry, Jesus then fell sound asleep.

Halfway across the unpredictable sea, the boat nearly capsized when a fierce storm suddenly arose.

Waves crashed over the sides of the boat and the disciples panicked. In the fury of the wind and rain and waves, they could picture only one scene—a quick trip to the bottom of the lake! In desperation they roused Jesus, who in a word reduced the storm to a gently shimmering sea. Then he rebuked the disciples with these words: "Why are you timid, you men of *little faith?*"

Why did the disciples have little faith? How did their faith differ from that of the centurion? The difference was that in the midst of the storm, the disciples forgot that Jesus had said, "We're going to the other side." They pictured themselves drowning, not reaching the dry land of the far shore. They mistakenly assumed that if they were going to arrive safely on the other side that they would enjoy smooth sailing along the way. They didn't anticipate such fierce trouble en route to their destination.

TREASURE IN EVERY TRIAL

Many of us make the same mistake. During difficult times we forget that God has promised to produce maturity, righteousness, and love through our trials. He has told us to "consider it all joy ... when you encounter various trials" (James 1:2) and that "we walk by faith, not by sight" (2 Corinthians 5:7). When waves threaten to capsize our boat, natural thinking takes over and we lose all hope of survival. People with inadequate faith say, "Those promises don't apply to me. God doesn't understand my situation. How can any good come out of all this suffering?" Years after a tragedy, they are lying helplessly at the bottom of the lake covered with barnacles of bitterness instead of walking on the sunny, sandy shore enjoying the fullness of God's blessing.

Many people I counsel suffer from a negative self-image because of the hardships they have endured. Discovering the treasure buried in our trials is the fastest way I know to raise self-worth. God wants us to think well of ourselves because He wants us to love others as we love ourselves. When we devalue ourselves, we hinder our love for others.

Treasure hunting can raise self-worth, no matter what the circumstances.

DISCOVERING TREASURE IN TRIALS

The following exercise is the one I use to discover the treasure in my personal trials. Perhaps it will work for you as well.

Divide a piece of paper into five columns and label the columns as follows: 1) What I like about myself; 2) My past trials; 3) Support people; 4) Benefits from trials; 5) Love in action. In the first column list at least three things you like about yourself.

In the second column list the things you don't like about yourself, the things that cause low self-worth. These are the painful experiences that cause anger, bitterness, and varying levels of grief. Some people have told me it's too painful to write down all their trials at one time, so you may prefer to focus on one or two for the moment and deal with others at another time.

In the third column list the people who have helped you through your more serious trials. Something in your past may have been so painful that you needed a professional counselor. Or perhaps you found a friend who prayed with you until you regained your strength after a particularly difficult experience.

In the fourth column list whatever benefits you can think of that came as a result of your trial. If you can't think of any at first, remember that for Christians all trials produce various aspects of love, so think of ways a trial has helped you to better love God, yourself, or others.

In the final column list ways in which the benefits of column four have changed your behavior. The purpose of trials is not just for our own self-worth, but so that we might love others as well. The two greatest commandments are that we love God and one another. So this final column shows how the value we've gained from trials can be used to help others.

You may still doubt that your own trials have any buried treasure, so let's look at some examples. I'll start with my own chart and illustrate how some of my painful experiences have turned into treasures. (See chart.)

Joy That Lasts

TREASURE HUNT

What I Like About Myself	Past Trials	Support People	Benefits from Trials	Love in Action

COLUMN ONE: WHAT I LIKE ABOUT MYSELF

In the first column I wrote that I like my family life, some of my speaking skills, my concern for helping people, the fulfillment I've found in God's love and joy, and the overflow of ministering to others through seminars, books, and films. (This is a very personal list, so if you prefer to keep some things confidential use a numerical code as I have done.)

COLUMN TWO: TRIALS

In the next column, second only to my experience with Dale, I wrote flunking third grade. I've been embarrassed by that for years, and my kids still tease me about it. They wonder how anyone with half a brain could flunk third grade. But now I can smile about it because I've found the treasure in it. Another trial was the time I expected a $2,000 refund on my income taxes, only to learn that I owed $1,700 instead! List whatever *you* consider a trial, even though others may think it insignificant. (Again, you might want to use code.)

COLUMN THREE: SUPPORT PEOPLE

During my trial with Dale my feelings were so intense that without the help of some close Christian friends my recovery would have taken much longer. So in column three I list the people God brought into my life to encourage and help me. Over a period of two years, much of that support came in my meetings with Jim and through the love of a small group of Christian friends.

COLUMN FOUR: BENEFITS

Although extremely painful, I can say now that the benefits of my experience with Dale have been so great that I would go through it again for the treasures of love I discovered.

Empathy and compassion. Because of the rejection I felt, I now have tremendous empathy for couples going through a divorce. I understand the agony of rejection and separation when the situation is beyond control. My eyes often fill with tears when I listen to a man or woman in a painful relationship. I want so desperately to help them discover what I've learned. Compassion is another important part of love, and it's learned through trials (2 Corinthians 1:5–7). I also have a much better understanding of those in midlife crisis, which is probably what I was experiencing during those two years.

Renewed appreciation and love for Norma. Through all my trials, Norma held tightly to me and helped hold our family together.

A deeper sense of love and forgiveness. When I realized how selfish I had been and yet how my Lord and my family still forgave me, my love and forgiveness for others increased significantly.

Patience. Until my experience with Dale I always expected things to happen quickly. During this crisis I had no choice but to wait.

Wisdom. I learned what God's priorities for life really are—to love Him and others!

Love and acceptance. These have been the greatest benefits of all. My experience with Dale forced me to depend on Christ alone for love and acceptance. I hate to think of how many more years I might have wasted if I had continued to look to Dale or to any other person, possession, position, or place for fulfillment. Because I was humbled through this experience, I gained the greatest gift, an understanding of God's grace, which gives me the power to love others.

Humility was a benefit of flunking third grade. Not being promoted with my friends kept me humble for many years. To this day I am self-conscious about my spelling, especially if I have to write a note to one of my kid's teachers, because my atrocious spelling was one of the reasons I was held back. Even though my spelling has improved, I'm still embarrassed sometimes by words I carelessly misspell. I know, however, that being a better speller will not give me fulfillment. So whenever embarrassment strikes I thank God that His grace reflected in my weakness makes me a more loving person.

Flunking third grade also made it difficult for me to read aloud in front of people. One of my most embarrassing moments was being unable to finish reading a section of Scripture at my church when I was president of a large college group. That experience humbled me and gave me a deep concern for those struggling with dyslexia and other spelling and reading disorders. Also, because I was so embarrassed, I am extremely careful to not embarrass people who attend my marriage seminars. My embarrassment increased my sensitivity, a requirement for a loving person.

What about the benefits of owing the IRS $1,700 instead of it owing me $2,000? The first benefit was the reminder that money gives no fulfillment. Although we had to sacrifice to pay the extra money, I knew that neither the money nor anything we could buy with it could add anything to my knowledge of God. Second, we had to trust God to meet our needs. Third, the trial forced me to get professional help and learn to better manage our finances.

COLUMN FIVE: LOVE IN ACTION

The treasures I found through my problems with Dale gave me an opportunity to minister around the country. What I learned has been the basis for two books about marriage, a parenting book, a series of cassette tapes, the seminars I teach, a six-part film series, and many counseling opportunities.

The embarrassment of flunking third grade has made me more patient with my kids in regard to their schoolwork. Instead of reacting harshly if their grades aren't what I expect, I try to understand what caused the problem so I can help them succeed. Also, I'm more patient with those who struggle with low self-esteem, no matter what the reason.

I've often used the example of the tax miscalculations to encourage others to go to God alone as their source of life.

I could add many other trials to my list, but I don't want to leave the impression that this concept works only for me. Let's look at how it has worked in others' lives.

8

Thinking My Trial Is an Exception

"THAT'S FINE FOR YOU," some may say, "but you don't know my problems. Surely there can't be any treasure in my situation."

Are there exceptions to this principle? After counseling with hundreds of individuals, I have yet to find a single one. Sometimes we have to dig deep, but the treasure is always there. Sometimes the treasure is coated with corrosion, but if we do some scraping we begin to see its value. And a glimpse of the first sparkle of gold keeps us scraping until the shiny nugget is free from its ugly coating. The best scraper is thanksgiving. Thanksgiving expresses our faith that God can indeed bring treasures out of our trials by producing love in us, and faith adds muscle to the scraping process, even in the worst of trials.

JILL—A SHATTERED LIFE MADE WHOLE

Jill was born into a wealthy family, but when she was three years old her father deserted the family, leaving her mother and brothers destitute. As a young girl she was raped by her uncle, then her brothers. As a teenager and young woman, she struggled through a number of relationships with males who took advantage of her sexually. She finally married, but the scars of her traumatic past remained.

In our first encounter, we spent two hours treasure hunting. When I asked Jill to state what she liked about herself, she couldn't think of a single thing. With some encouragement, she finally said she liked her blond hair, her loving husband, their pretty little daughter, and her college degree. Her trials were the repeated incidents of incest and rape and her father's rejection.

She particularly needed support concerning her father. She could not understand how someone so wealthy could reject his family and leave them penniless. Most of the time she took it personally, feeling that he had actually rejected her. She needed someone who could pray with her and help her talk through this trauma. She needed to see her father as a man with his own hurts and struggles, and ultimately she needed to forgive him. I assured her that forgiveness would come in time, but until then, she needed a friend or counselor to help her work toward that freedom.

We began to look for treasure in her trials. I had to prompt her at first, but gradually she began to see the love God had given her through what her family had done out of their own selfishness. She hated to see anyone misused, even on television, and she was extremely sensitive to injustice. Her deep empathy for others helped her raise her daughter. She was very careful who she used for baby-sitters and was doubly alert to even minor offenses toward her child.

Her sensitivity, which was highly refined because of the verbal abuse she received as a child, made her always careful to not hurt or mislead people with her words. She also had a realistic view of men, which she would use to educate her daughter. Even with her husband, who was a very gentle and caring man, she was alert to anything that might be interpreted as child abuse. Her cautiousness helped her husband be a more sensitive and loving mate and father. Jill also had an ability to spot abused women and children simply by the look on their faces. She was very aware of the social problems of incest and wife- and child-abuse.

The greatest benefit she received was her relationship with Jesus Christ. The repeated violation of her body had totally humiliated her and driven her into Christ's waiting arms. I reminded her that the greater our embarrassment from circumstances beyond our control, the more God's grace is available. "That's true!" she admitted. "Often I've gone running to Christ's arms and found great comfort there." She realized Christ understood how she felt, for He was physically and verbally abused and humiliated by His public beating and execution on a cross. Jill's dependency on Christ gave her supernatural grace to live and inner power that many never know.

God transformed Jill's trial into a treasure in a

remarkable demonstration of love in action. Her painful past enables her to minister to teenage victims of incest and child abuse in a way few others can. They listen to her because they know she understands them. She emphasizes to the girls their great value, and gradually their self-worth rises as they witness her unconditional love and concern for them. From there she leads them on their own treasure hunt through their trials and on to a loving heavenly Father who gives them a blessing, not a curse.

Let me emphasize again that although good can *come out* of tragedy, that does not mean the tragic act is good. As Paul said in Romans 6, God's grace is applied to sin, but we do not sin that grace may abound. Woe to the man who would rape or abuse anyone (Luke 17:1). But when an evil act is committed against us, God's love is available for healing and growth.

Complete healing usually requires a grieving process. Immediately after a tragedy, the victim needs comfort from loving, sensitive people. Regret usually sets in next, followed by denial and an attempt to minimize the tragedy. Finally, after weeks or months, comes the willingness to treasure hunt. Although we can begin to treasure hunt immediately after a trial, and sometimes even during a trial, most of us need time to regain our strength before we begin the emotionally draining digging process.

DENISE—SELF-WORTH RESTORED

Treasure hunting is important because it can also build self-esteem. Seventeen-year-old Denise hadn't suffered any experiences as traumatic as Jill's, but constant conflict with her parents continually reinforced her poor self-image. Denise challenged me after a seminar, stating that she knew there were no benefits in the things she'd endured. "I'm always looking for the first exception," I said to her. "Why don't we sit down and you tell me your problems."

I quickly learned from Denise that she hated four things about her life: she believed she was ugly, stupid, and overweight, and she was convinced her parents were unfair.

"Do you want God's best in your life?" I asked her.

"Yes," she answered.

"What do you think God's best is?"

"I really don't know."

"God's best and highest will is for us to love (value) Him with all our hearts, and to love (value) others as ourselves. Do you realize that you have everything you need to fulfill God's will and experience His best in your life?

"And just how can I find it?" she inquired.

We started with her problems concerning her physical appearance. I asked her if she wanted to be beautiful.

"Of course!" she snapped.

I explained that a humble attitude was the key to physical beauty because God gives His grace to the humble. I suggested that she pray a prayer like this: "Lord, thank You that through love You can give me spiritual beauty that will reflect on my physical appearance. Even though I think I'm unattractive now, thank You that as You teach me how to love You and others, people will begin to see Your beauty in me."

Then I suggested that perhaps God was using her appearance to protect her. She seemed puzzled, so I explained further. Because of her appearance, men would not be attracted to her for purely physical reasons, and she would not be tempted to use her appearance to manipulate people. So in any relationship, whether friendship or romance, she would know the person was attracted to her because of her inner, lasting qualities that only God could develop within her.

She smiled for the first time, and her smile revealed a pretty face. Simply relaxing her facial muscles immediately made her more attractive. When a person can thank God for the good they know is there but cannot yet see, facial expressions often change and others can see a new beauty and calm.

I went on to explain that self-hatred might be the cause of her overeating. If she started to relax and began to like herself, the compulsion to overeat might subside. But even if she could not lose weight, she could still find her fulfillment in God.

Denise's below-average intelligence also held a disguised benefit. Denise had never battled with God over theological issues. For her, a childlike faith was more natural. Although asking God difficult questions about our faith is not wrong, there is value in simple faith, as Jesus showed when He used a child as an example.

As we talked, Denise realized this was true. She told me of a number of times when students at her high school had sought her counsel because she was known for being trusting and for having above-average common sense.

We then considered Denise's relationship with her parents. Any support she received from them was based solely on her achievements, which were few. Denise believed they preferred her brother because he excelled in athletics and earned good grades in school. The concept of unconditional love and affection was foreign to the family. Her father traveled extensively, which Denise resented, and her mother complained about having to raise the kids without his help.

Each of these trials had its benefits. Because Denise felt unloved, her sensitivity to others from similar homes was unusually strong. I explained how that sensitivity could, if she would let it, enable her to reach out to others, to accept them as they are, and to understand their needs. Her parents' favoritism revealed the futility and frustration of expecting people to make her happy. Learning this could lead her into a closer relationship with Christ, who would never leave her or forsake her. And her father's frequent absences turned out to be the greatest benefit of all. Her need for a father was the major factor that brought her to faith in Christ. And finally, her poor relationship with her parents could make her more sensitive to her own children when she married.

Denise skipped away from our meeting with a smile on her face. Several years after our meeting she sent me a letter telling me what good things God was continuing to do in her life. She had gone on to college, majored in sociology, and become a social worker helping the handicapped. Her trials, she said, produced the patience she needed for this kind of work, so now she too helps people discover treasure in their trials. *The more love she gives, the more her self-worth soars.*

The apostle Paul understood this mystery when he wrote his famous explanation of love: "Love is patient, love is kind, and is not jealous; love does not brag and is not arrogant, does not act unbecomingly; it does not seek its own, is not provoked, does not take into account a wrong suffered, does not rejoice in unrighteousness, but rejoices with the truth; *bears all things, believes all things, hopes all things, endures all things*" (1 Corinthians 13:4–7). These qualities of mature love are given to us through trials (see James 1:2; Hebrews 12:10–11).

DAVID—FROM REJECTION TO ACCEPTANCE

David was a successful real estate broker when his wife left him and moved with their two young daughters to a city 2,200 miles away. The emotional pain of rejection hurt so badly that David couldn't believe me when I told him we could find a benefit in his trial. We looked at Hebrews 12:11: "All discipline for the moment seems not to be joyful, but sorrowful; yet to those who have been *trained* by it [the discipline], afterwards it yields the peaceful fruit of righteousness." I explained to him how this trial could, if he was willing, make him more righteous, which meant he would be more Christlike, which meant he would also be more loving.

As we talked, David realized that his actions had caused his wife to leave him. His priority had been his career rather than his family, so he had neglected those he loved. David's new priorities were the first benefit of his trial. Next he realized his self-centeredness and how he had been caught up in attaining material wealth, which he knew could never give him a fulfilling life. His family wanted *him*, not more of his wealth. This experience forced Dave to see that no aspect of God's creation could give him lasting satisfaction.

Even though Dave failed to provide the love his family needed before they moved away, his concern for his daughters was genuine. He wondered how they would adjust to a new city, and particularly how their self-worth would be affected if they did not receive the love they needed. But it wasn't too late for Dave to start expressing his love. This trial showed him that he needed to communicate love to his wife and children. He started doing that in his phone conversations and letters, and he enlisted the help of an older Christian couple to help him learn practical ways of expressing love. The more he learned about how to love, and actually put that love into action, the more his self-worth improved.

BIBLICAL EXAMPLES OF TREASURE HUNTING

Scripture abounds with examples of good coming out of evil situations. We shudder at the injustice meted out to Jacob's son Joseph. Out of jealousy, his brothers sold him into slavery. Then, after he had risen to prominence in Potiphar's household, he was unjustly accused by Potiphar's wife and thrown in prison. But many years later Joseph was able to say to his repentant brothers, *"You meant evil against me, but God meant it for good* in order to bring about this present result, to preserve many people alive"* (Genesis 50:20).

David was another victim of jealousy. King Saul, on hearing that David was to replace him as king, set out to destroy him and foil God's plan. Enraged, insane, and jealous, the king hunted his one-time friend and counselor for years through the wilderness. The experience, though bitter at the time, made David a better king.

Peter, although humiliated when he denied Christ three times, turned that distasteful experience into a powerful treasure that enabled him to follow Christ's command to "feed My sheep."

The greatest example of all is Jesus Christ Himself who suffered unjustly and was executed in one of the most humiliating manners ever devised. That tragedy has become the basis for our greatest joy—the hope of eternal life. The author of Hebrews expressed this truth when he wrote, "Although He was a Son, He learned obedience from the things which He suffered. And having been made perfect, He became to all those who obey Him the source of eternal salvation" (Hebrews 5:8–9) and ". . . fixing our eyes on Jesus, the author and perfecter of faith, who for the joy set before Him endured the cross, despising the shame . . ." (Hebrews 12:2).

Christ knew that after He suffered, we would enjoy the treasure of salvation.

We could look at many more examples of people who have found treasure in their hurts and suffering. Perhaps you're going through a problem right now and you can't find any treasure. Work through your own chart. If you still can't find it, thank God that it is there even though you don't see it yet. In fact, thanksgiving is one of the best ways to discover the benefits of a trial because it expresses our faith in God's promise that good can be found in all we suffer (see Isaiah 61:3).

Faith is trusting that God's Word is reliable. If He promises, "We are going to the other side," then we are going to the other side. Many promises in Scripture can sustain us in our trials. They are the equivalent of Christ's promise to the disciples. Here are some of God's promises that assure us we will get to the other side and find treasure.

"God causes all things to work together for *good* to those who love God, to those who are called according to His purpose [which is to love others]" (Romans 8:28). Almost every trial increases our love for others. So even though we may not immediately see any other good, we know of at least one—more love.

"In everything give thanks; for this is God's will

for you in Christ Jesus" (1 Thessalonians 5:18). We can thank God *during* our painful circumstances because we know love is hidden in the pain.

"Consider it all joy, my brethren, when you encounter various trials; knowing that the testing of your faith produces endurance" (James 1:2–3). Trials are our friends because they produce maturity, eventually making us "complete, lacking in nothing."

"[God] disciplines us for our good, that we may share His holiness. All discipline for the moment seems not to be joyful, but sorrowful; yet to those who have been trained by it, afterwards it yields the peaceful fruit of righteousness" (Hebrews 12:10–11). Righteousness means right living and is summed up in loving God and others (Matthew 22:37–40).

"The goal of our instruction is love" (1 Timothy 1:5). Once again we see that love, life's highest purpose, is God's goal for us, and the Bible equates maturity with love (1 John 4:11–12).

You may be getting the impression that we can only learn to love through trials. Not true. We can short-circuit trials by humbling ourselves. Christ stated, "Whoever exalts himself shall be humbled; and whoever humbles himself shall be exalted" (Matthew 23:12). One reason the genuinely humble are lifted up is because God honors those who love. I prefer to humble myself and avoid trials and discipline whenever possible. Avoiding trials completely, however, is impossible.

No one likes trials, yet no one can escape them. We can let them ruin our lives—make us bitter, angry, and resentful—or we can look for the treasure that will let us love and serve others.

By allowing trials to draw us to God, our cups will not only be full but will be on the brink of overflow—the continual experience of those who know and do the greatest commandment: love God and others.

9

Gaining a Clear Purpose in Life

TERRY NEVER ANTICIPATED that his boss, who was also his close friend, would lay him off after twenty-two years with the company. As vice president of one of America's largest truck-rental companies, Terry had just returned from an out-of-state training conference when he was told the shocking news.

"Why, God, did you let this happen?" Terry asked. His friends encouraged him to treasure-hunt, but the only benefit Terry could find was that he had a lot more time for his family. Within a month another national truck-rental firm hired him, only to release him six weeks later.

Most of us can relate to Terry's disappointment. We too wonder about God's plan and direction and how we can know if we are really in the center of His will.

God's Word addresses these questions directly. In fact, Scripture specifically states God's will for each of us. The power of this truth motivates and energizes us and adds creativity and excitement to any endeavor. It can pull us out of bed in the morning with renewed enthusiasm. It tells us when we're in the center of God's will, gives us a sense of purpose, and adds to our self-worth. It can even help us find, or live successfully with, our mate.

What is God's will? A lawyer once asked Jesus that same question. Jesus told him that God's highest will, the greatest commandment, was to "Love the Lord your God with all your heart, and with all your soul, and with all your mind" (Matthew 22:37–38). Then he added the second greatest commandment: "You shall love your neighbor as yourself." That pretty well covers it all; everything else required by God flows from these two commandments.

> *Obedience to the first commandment fills us; obedience to the second makes us overflow with motivation, creativity, and excitement about life.*

Seeing people renewed, healed, blessed, encouraged, and motivated by our love for them increases our self-worth, and that starts the overflow in our lives.

People frequently ask me how to find God's specific will about such things as who they should marry, what vocation they should pursue, whether or not they should change jobs or careers. For years I had similar questions. Since 1978, however, I've known God's will for me and have eagerly watched it materialize.

I believe God has something for each of us to accomplish. I've simplified the process of understanding and practicing God's will with a system I call the *FIVE M's*. If you or someone you know wants to "nail down" God's will, this simple five-point plan might help. Picture a circle with the word *Master* in the center. The words *Mission, Method, Maintenance,* and *Mate* surround it like four points on a compass.

The five M's illustrate both elements of God's will—loving God and loving others—by asking five questions. *Master* asks, "Who am I going to live for?" *Mission* asks, "What does God want me to do?" *Method* asks, "How will I fulfill my mission?" *Maintenance* asks, "How will I evaluate and adjust my methods?" And *Mate* asks, "Do we agree about our mission?"

Notice that Master is the first and most important aspect of God's will. The other four elements relate to God's second command. When all five parts work in harmony, we experience the overflowing life promised to those in the center of God's will.

MASTER—WHO AM I LIVING FOR?

The first M asks if I am living for my own self-centered desires or for God. We covered this in the first six chapters. Acknowledging God as the source of my life means that I treasure Him and His ways above all else. Phrased as a prayer it says: "God I love You. I commit my life to You one hundred percent. I understand that Your highest will for me is to love You and to love others as I love myself. You said that if we obey these commandments, we are fulfilling all the laws of Scripture (Matthew 22:40). I am committed to doing that, whatever it takes."

New Testament writers agree that loving God and loving others are the highest commandments, the royal decree, the law of God. Paul writes that one word—love—fulfills the whole law (Galatians 5:14). John says we prove our love for God by loving others (1 John 4:7–8). And James says we do well if we fulfill the royal law, "You shall love your neighbor as yourself" (James 2:8).

A basic principle about my own life can be summed up in one sentence: I realize I'm a "10" to God, but I choose to value God and others higher than I do myself (see Philippians 2:3–4). The highest position I can ever attain is to be a servant to God and others.

In the last chapter, we saw how God buries treasures in our trials. Through persistent digging we can find the gems of love, but using it for our own fulfillment and satisfaction is only part of the plan; the second half of God's law requires us to *invest* our newfound treasure in the lives of others.

MISSION—WHAT DOES GOD WANT ME TO DO?

Since God is our master, asking Him what He wants us to do in regard to loving people starts the process that uncovers our basic purpose for living. While Christ fills us, we are to search for ways to express His love to others, which is what it means to discover our mission.

Learning what people need and looking for creative ways to meet those needs unlocks the door to all successful relationships and enterprises. Those who learn the secret of serving people's real needs are the most successful. We can take this principle much deeper, however. Many people succeed in serving others, but for self-centered motives. We've already examined the futility of such efforts. Genuine fulfillment comes only through knowing and loving God first and then through serving others in response to His love.

It took two years to learn God's specific purpose for me after I stopped working for Dale. I used this four-point checklist to determine my mission in life.

I CONSULTED SCRIPTURE.

As I read the Bible, passages about relationships jumped out at me as though God was drawing my attention to them. In Isaiah 58 I read phrases like "to let the oppressed go free" and to "break every yoke." The words "rebuild the ancient ruins" made me think immediately of how Christ could rebuild ruined families. I used this passage as a basis for many hours of prayer.

When I read Luke 4, where Jesus said He was the fulfillment of the prophecy in Isaiah 61, my heart leaped: "The Spirit of the Lord is upon Me, because He anointed Me to preach the gospel to the poor. He has sent Me to proclaim release to the captives, and recovery of sight to the blind, to set free those who are downtrodden." The words *release* and *set free* caught my attention. The Hebrew words from which they are translated are the basis of the word *forgiveness*, which means to untie someone so he can be restored. That's what I wanted to do—untie people from the knots that kept them from experiencing full and meaningful relationships.

I proceeded carefully in this process because I do not advocate pointing to isolated verses and stating, "This is God's verse for me." I went further by seeking God and waiting for His peace after I had checked as many facts in Scripture as possible.

While studying Scripture I also kept my eyes open to the world around me and saw that some of society's greatest needs were in family relationships. Experts confirmed my observations. Over and over they testified that family deterioration was one of the major problems in the United States.

I PRAYED THAT I WOULD HAVE GOD'S DESIRES.

God has promised to give us the desires of our heart if we delight in Him (Psalm 37:4), so as I read passages about relationships I prayed, "Lord, is this Your heartbeat? Is this what You want me to do? I only want to follow Your plan."

As I prayed, read Scripture, and heard about the thousands of crumbling homes, I began to sense how God felt about this problem. With that understanding came a desire to help do something about it.

I SOUGHT THE COUNSEL OF FRIENDS.

In addition to searching Scripture and praying, I quizzed others about what they imagined me doing for the rest of my life. I encouraged them to not limit their thinking to what they already knew about my knowledge and skills. Norma immediately responded by saying, "I see you doing something different than what you're doing today." Even while I was still working with Dale, she often told me she didn't think I was in the right spot because I was doing more administration than counseling, and counseling and speaking, she thought, were my strengths. I'm sad to have to admit that I ignored her input for many years.

One day a close friend stopped by my house to say he had been praying for me. He knew of my struggle to determine God's plan as to how I could demonstrate His love for people. When he said he felt impressed to read Isaiah 58 to me, I felt my eyes open wide. Of all the Scriptures he could have selected. "I see you releasing oppressed families and breaking every yoke that binds families in disharmony." Then he added, "I know this passage doesn't refer specifically to you, but when I read it I saw you jetting around the world, strengthened by the Lord with the heritage of Jacob."

Eventually all who knew me well reinforced what I was already learning from Scripture. Then one day my close friend Jim Stewart, a real estate broker and developer, drove me around town to see the various lots he was developing. As we rode, I summarized what I felt God was leading me to do.

"I've been praying about you and how I can help families through what I do," Jim said. "Much of my time is spent developing and selling commercial and residential buildings, so maybe what I can do is to help finance your work."

When our church personnel committee met to consider my future, their enthusiasm compounded my own. They even wanted to ask the church to help finance my mission. And so it went. Person after person corroborated what I sensed God was calling me to do.

Checking with all these people confirmed to me that my goal was not selfish, that I was not anxious for personal gain or loss. My relationship with Christ met all my needs for personal worth and achievement, so I prayed, "Lord, I'm already satisfied with You—You are filling my life. Now show me what You want me to do for others." Although I trusted God to reveal His plan in His time, the number of lives shattering around me countered my patience with a sense of urgency. So I kept saying, "Hurry up, Lord. But take Your time."

I TESTED MY PEACE.

A fourth test of knowing God's mission was His peace in my heart. When I was nearly certain that my desires matched what God wanted me to do, I thanked Him that He would be faithful to answer my request. I stood in His prayer line each day, knowing He would reveal His specific will for me. Then I waited for the peace of God that surpasses all comprehension (Philippians 4:7), which I knew would guard my heart and mind in the Lord and keep me from doubting, fretting, or continually questioning.

Sometimes I pretended I was teaching a conference. As I did, I examined myself to see if I had peace about it. Or I envisioned myself working in a counseling center, going through a whole week of appointments. What type of people would I see? Depressed and despairing parents? Misunderstood husbands and wives? Lonely singles? When I imagined myself helping husbands and wives find restoration with the Lord and harmony with each other, I had tremendous peace and excitement.

Finally I knew my mission: to mend broken relationships between people and between people and God. Specifically, I committed myself to love God and my family first, and on the basis of those relationships to teach others what I was learning and to help them discover their own mission and method. Today my mission statement is "to enthusiastically motivate others to highly value God, others, and themselves."

Unfortunately, many people make crucial decisions about the next step, method, which includes education and career, without stopping to determine their mission. I believe this is one reason for the proliferation of mid-life crises. It may also be a reason some people don't finish their education. College is a method, and a college education has much more value if we know our mission.

METHOD—HOW WILL I FULFILL MY MISSION?

Some people enjoy seeking God's will, but hesitate to move when He reveals it. But knowing our mission, although an imperative first step, is only the beginning. After testing it to be sure it's right, we need to move through open doors to fulfill it. First we need to evaluate the variety of possible methods to accomplish our mission. Here are some examples of missions and methods:

This is where the fun and adventure really begins. Part of the enjoyment of pursuing methods is realizing that our natural abilities are not the only criteria for determining whether or not to use a particular method. With enough study, time, and experience, and by drawing upon the power of the Holy Spirit, we can excel in almost any field.

Suppose a woman's mission is to relieve people of physical pain. She could do a variety of things to accomplish her mission: become a medical doctor or dentist, work for the Red Cross, raise money to send medical teams to third-world countries, do research to discover new pain-relieving drugs, become a paramedic, a nurse, or a physical therapist, etc.

MISSION (What I'll do in life)	METHOD (How I'll do it)
Relieve people of physical pain.	Doctor Dentist Nurse Physical therapist Hospital administrator Pharmacist Relief worker
Feed those who are hungry.	Restaurant (owner or worker) Missionary Grocery store (owner or worker) World hunger relief
Provide shelter for people.	Building contractor Remodeler Interior decorator Motel operator Builder of inexpensive homes for poor
Reach the unreached for Christ.	Missionary Airplane pilot Preacher Tract writer Crusade team member Film producer Evangelist

To carry out my mission of strengthening relationships I had an unlimited number of methods to choose from. I could teach seminars, counsel, become a pastor, disciple couples, become a psychologist or social worker, serve as a chaplain in a hospital, etc.

The process of eliminating methods is as difficult as thinking of them. One thing I did (which, incidentally, I continue to do to keep my skills sharp) was to ask experts how they thought I could accomplish my mission. For example, I talked with successful writers to learn what makes some books better than others; I studied popular speakers to learn what makes them effective; and I read books and periodicals to stay current on the latest insights in counseling. Throughout this process I tried not to rush God, but I didn't want to wait any longer than necessary to begin fulfilling His call.

Christian psychologist Dr. Henry Brandt strongly influenced my choice of methods. In 1978, while teaching a conference with him in the Virgin Islands, I told him what I believed God wanted me to do, and he gave me this fantastic advice: "Gary," he said, "I've used a lot of methods to help couples in my thirty years of ministry, and I've concluded that five of them are the best for ministering to people in difficult relationships. The first one helps the most people. The others follow in descending order of effectiveness."

1. Write a book. This method scared me. How could someone who has difficulty spelling ever write a book. But Dr. Brandt was emphatic. "You'll help more people more effectively by forcing yourself to clarify your message through the printed word," he

said. "And you'll help people you'd never meet otherwise."

2. Record my messages on tape. This method offered a little more hope. By refining my messages and recording them on cassettes I could make them available all over the world.

3. Record my refined messages on film or videotape. The more specialized my message became, the more strongly he felt about my need to investigate this possibility. Initially I sensed that this too was something I could never do.

4. Speak in churches, conferences, and seminars. Although Dr. Brandt encouraged me to use this method, he warned me that I would help fewer people through this method than through the first three. He agreed, however, that there is tremendous power and effectiveness in preaching.

5. Counsel on a personal basis. This method, although highly effective, helps the least number of people. Dr. Brandt advised me to set up regular counseling sessions, however, because without contact with real people and real problems I'd soon have nothing to say through the other four methods.

In ways beyond my ability to imagine, God eventually opened all five of these doors for me. Within six years from the time I first began "standing in God's line," God began to supernaturally answer all five. At first I eliminated the thought of writing a book or making a movie. Considering my literary abilities and my financial resources, I felt these were out of the question. But the more I thought about how all things are possible through Christ who strengthens us (Philippians 4:13) and that it was God who wanted me to serve people, I concluded that my attitude limited God. The more I prayed about and studied the five methods Dr. Brandt suggested—books, tapes, movies, speaking, and counseling—the more I sensed a peace about using all five methods myself.

Norma was as excited about the five methods as I was, so together with our children and a few friends we began to pray that before I turned sixty God would allow me to write a book about helping couples stay in harmony. Like the widow in Luke 18, I started every morning in God's line, praying and hoping for the day I would see a book in print. Sometimes I walked into bookstores and imagined my book on the shelf, even though I knew my skills were still inadequate. I didn't expect God to answer my prayer for a number of years, but that didn't diminish my enthusiasm.

While I was standing in God's line many people tried to discourage me by reminding me of how many books have already been written about marriage and of how difficult it is to get a book published. Then they would say, "And almost none of them become bestsellers." They were right; the odds are slim that any one book will sell more than an average number of copies. They also tried to discourage me from doing a film series because of the popularity of the James Dobson films.

I countered their pessimism and my doubts with the assurance that God was leading me into this. Since He had a unique message to give me, it didn't matter how many books and films were already available. Besides, millions of people needed to be reached, so God could use as many people as He wanted to help.

I knew I needed a lot of preparation. Whatever your mission and whatever methods you choose to accomplish it, you must learn the necessary skills, even though it may take years. Don't limit yourself and God by dwelling on what you already know and can do. We learn best by doing—over and over and over—and if we are faithful in preparing, we will be ready when the opportunity comes. I wanted to be ready when the opportunity came. In other words, as a good friend of mine says, "If God promises you a horse, you'd better start learning to ride!"

Only six months after I started praying, God nearly knocked me off my feet with His reply. My friend Steve Scott called from Philadelphia and asked if I would let his company finance *two* books by me. He would help me write them and Pat Boone would endorse them in an advertisement on national television.

Ephesians 3:20 flashed through my mind: "Now to Him who is able to do exceeding abundantly *beyond* all that we ask or think ..." I had prayed for one book, but God gave me an opportunity to write two. I had dreamed of getting one title into bookstores, but God wanted to market my books to a much larger audience through television.

I accepted the opportunity enthusiastically, even though I still considered myself the least likely candidate to write a book. But God is not limited by our inabilities. He does his best work with people who are willing and available to carry out His will of loving others. Willingness is the key; knowledge and skills can be learned.

Although I was a willing student, I had no idea of the amount of time and effort learning required. That was especially true of my first two books. Each day I felt as if I were being whipped with a belt. Many times I wondered why I had allowed myself to get into such a pressurized situation—having to produce two books in only a short time. Many days I simply concluded, "God, since You opened this door, and because I know You're faithful to Your children, I believe You'll enable me to finish what You've started. But I want You to know that this is a miserable and painful experience."

While working on the two books, I continued to pray about the other four methods. Before I had finished writing, a producer from Hollywood, California, called to ask if he could send a film crew to Texas to make me part of a movie they were producing on strengthening families. In my busyness, I turned down the opportunity without really praying about it. Besides, I'd never heard of the featured pastor in the film, a man by the name of Charles Swindoll. The film, *Strike the Original Match*, as everyone knows by now, became an award winner that still ministers to thousands around the world. God had opened the door I was pounding on, and I had slammed it in His face.

That experience taught me an important lesson. From then on when I knocked, I kept my eyes on the door, expecting it to open any minute. I felt like the Christians in the Book of Acts must have felt when they failed to recognize answered prayer. They were so preoccupied with praying for Peter's release from prison that they didn't believe the servant who told them he was knocking on their door. Since turning down the opportunity to participate in "Strike the Original Match," I've paid much more attention to open doors. For each opportunity I try to discern my "serving capacity" and God's will.

Other methods besides these five have also opened up, including opportunities on various television and radio programs. On some occasions I have felt such intense pressure that seconds before the program begins I can barely remember my name, much less the answers to any questions. In those final seconds, while listening to the director count down, I close my eyes and say, "Okay, Lord, here we go. I don't know how it will go, but I'm doing this to help people. If I embarrass anyone, including You, thank You ahead of time for the massive doses of grace I'll receive because of how humble I'll feel. I know Your grace will enable me to be a more loving person, which is Your ultimate will."

MAINTENANCE—ARE MY METHODS STILL EFFECTIVE?

Once we have recognized our mission and are actively pursuing several methods, we'll begin to see which methods are most effective and concentrate on those. In addition, we need to continually ask God to reveal any other methods He wants us to use to communicate the message He's given us.

The first time I heard James Dobson's radio program "Focus on the Family," I realized it would be an effective vehicle to communicate the message God had given me. When I heard reports about the size of Dobson's audience throughout the world, I got in line before the Lord and asked Him for a chance to be a guest so I could share some of the principles of marriage I'd written in my two books.

The opportunity finally came through a parenting book I'd written, not the marriage books, but by this time God's unexpected tactics didn't surprise me as much as they did at first. I enjoyed the interaction with Gill Moegerle and Dr. Dobson and thought the interview went well—until I heard a recording of it. Hearing myself constantly interrupting Jim and Gill embarrassed me. The technique of "actively listening" that is so effective in individual encounters was an embarrassing liability on radio. Almost every time they spoke, I made a noise or comment. It was so noticeable that numerous friends from around the country pointed it out to me.

In humility I went back to God and thanked Him for the opportunity. I recommitted my dedication to Him and to serving people. I told Him that even if I was never on another show, my life would be full by knowing Him.

Shortly afterward, John Nieder, the host for Dr. Howard Hendrick's radio program, flew to Phoenix to tape some programs with me. John had heard my interview with Dobson and he lovingly and sensitively instructed me on how to correct my problem. I made a sign and placed it on my desk during our interview:

DON'T TALK OR MAKE ANY NOISE WHILE JOHN IS
SPEAKING. Keeping quiet was difficult, but the mem-
ory of my previous humiliation silenced me. I
thanked God that He loved me enough to give me
another opportunity to learn the skills I needed to
communicate His message more effectively.

Soon after that I received the following letter:

> I'm writing to you to explain my changing
> feelings about you over the last several weeks.
> After I heard you on Dr. Dobson's program, I
> purposed that I would never listen to you again
> on radio because you interrupted Dr. Dobson so
> many times. A friend of mine called me the other
> day and said you were on Dr. Hendrick's pro-
> gram and it was helping her and I ought to tune
> in. I told her I could not listen to Mr. Smalley any
> more but if she wanted to, that was fine. But my
> curiosity got the better of me and I finally turned
> on the radio. To my amazement, you did not
> interrupt Mr. Nieder one time. I decided that you
> must have learned your lesson and I'm looking
> forward to hearing you again.

Any relationship, vocation, or ministry, if it is to
remain fresh and effective, needs continual evalu-
ation. Churches that continually reevaluate the times
they meet on Sunday, the programs they provide for
people, and even the method of sermon delivery, all
with the idea of better fulfilling their mission, usually
have the most exciting ministries. Unfortunately,
many get locked into a method and stay with it long
after it's served it's usefulness, which may indicate
they have either forgotten their mission or never
knew it.

MATE—DO WE AGREE ABOUT OUR MISSION?

The last M depends on whether we're single or married. For singles, this fits nicely as the final piece in God's plan for life. Once we know our master, mission, and methods, we are much better prepared to decide what type of person we should spend the rest of our lives with. (Or perhaps we may be better prepared to understand why God is calling us to remain single.) I'm not suggesting that marriage partners must have exactly the same mission and methods, but Scripture convinces me that God wants us as equally yoked as possible. I am grateful for a pastor who encouraged me to look for a wife who was going the same direction I was. During our marriage, Norma and I have remained enthusiastic teammates in our efforts to follow the will of God.

This conclusion may seem obvious, but many people believe they can marry simply on the basis of being "in love" with each other. Later they discover that their mate has a mission and several methods that are counterproductive to their own mission and methods.

For those who are married the last M concerns entering into ONENESS with our mate. Part of becoming one in marriage is learning to be of one mind. Unfortunately, many Christians determine their mission as if they were still single, never considering the effect it will have on their mate and children. Choosing a mission or a method without consulting family members can destroy a family. I've met writers who feel compelled to write regardless of the resistance they feel from their spouse or children. Mission and methods must be determined with our spouse if we're married. The oneness we gain is a tremendous asset to help us fulfill God's will. Because Norma and my children were part of the praying and planning process, they support my work when I have to be away from home or when I'm under a deadline. And they have the freedom to tell me when I need to get away from my work to spend more time with them.

The importance of oneness in marriage was demonstrated recently when I wanted to hire three additional staff members for our organization. Norma was against hiring any new staff; she wanted to continue as a Mom and Pop operation. She was afraid that hiring more people would take more of my time away from home. This disagreement forced us to reexamine our ministry and our time together as a family. After considering the family's needs first and together planning how to keep our family life healthy with an increased staff, we were able to bring on our first two employees. But we agreed to some guidelines so that each of Norma's concerns about our relationship and our family would be protected. As she saw my commitment to oneness with her, she remained as committed as I was to our mission and methods.

The five M's have proved to be the final ingredients in my search for the fulfilling life. For many years, I sought fulfillment not only from people and things, but from doing good, spiritual activities. Though my work helped people, my motivation was wrong; I expected worthwhile activities to fill my life.

When I recognized that activities, no matter how noble, could never permanently satisfy me, I began to allow God to fill me with His joy and love. That's when my needs were met. Free to serve others in love, I began to experience overflow, and with few exceptions, my joy has spilled over ever since.

10

Uncovering Six Secrets of Answered Prayer

WHEN I FIRST thought about writing this book, I intended it to help people learn to deal with trials and to see how Jesus Christ fills our life. Now, looking back over the first nine chapters, I realize I've written a book about building a relationship with God through prayer.

In chapter two, when I began my search for the source of life, I expressed my desire in a prayer: "God teach me what I am missing . . ." When I took my two-day personal retreat, all the lessons I learned through Scripture related to prayer. I realized that persistence—getting in God's line every day—was the secret of experiencing the fulfilling life God promised. Next I recognized that my negative emotions were warning lights that showed me I was expecting to find life's meaning in God's creation rather than in the Creator. Prayer corrected each of those emotions. Trials motivated me to treasure hunt—through prayer. And my search to find and implement God's mission and methods for my life led me even deeper in prayer.

Perhaps some of us think of prayer only as words of thanks we mutter before eating, as a ritual performed during a Sunday morning worship service, as clichés spoken during family devotions, or as cries for help in the face of a major crisis. These are valid occasions for prayer, but there is so much more. Prayer is what connects us to the source of life that fills us and makes life overflow.

Is it that simple? Is prayer all we need to have a fulfilling life? In some ways, a prayer life is like a puzzle made for preschoolers: it contains only a few pieces. Some people, however, delight in cutting each piece into smaller pieces so that it takes years of education and experience to assemble the puzzle. Although understanding increases as we mature, newborn believers can experience through prayer the joy of an overflowing life just as those who have known God for many years.

Although we could never explore every aspect of prayer in one chapter, or even in an entire book, the following thoughts explain what I believe it means to pray effectively.

PRAYER—REHEARSING GOD'S WILL

As the Israelites prepared to enter the Promised Land, Moses warned them not to forget all that God had commanded. Since Canaan had no thriving religious book publishing industry to preserve the law in writing, the Israelites taught God's commands to their children from morning until night—as they sat in their homes, as they walked to and from work, as they went to sleep, and as they rose in the morning (Deuteronomy 6:1–9). Every day they reviewed and reminded each other of God's laws.

Like the Israelites who rehearsed God's law, I believe prayer is rehearsing God's will. Regularly reminding ourselves of God's will keeps us pointed toward His goal and helps us learn what it means to value Him and others. It makes us ask questions like "Who am I going to love today? Who will I encourage? Have I offended anyone from whom I need to ask forgiveness?" It points out my selfishness and reveals my need to continually turn away from my selfish ways and show compassion to those around me by becoming a channel of God's love.

Rehearsing God's will also requires that I keep my mission in front of me. All successful corporations set clearly defined objectives that determine their day-to-day business strategy. Christ taught this principle in His Sermon on the Mount: "But seek first His kingdom and His righteousness; and all these things shall be added to you" (Matthew 6:33). I allow God to set the goals that will further His kingdom, then I go to Him daily, praying for the opportunities and resources to reach those objectives.

The most important aspect of rehearsing God's will is making sure that I pray only for things that are consistent with 1 Timothy 6:3–4: "If anyone advocates a different doctrine, and does not agree with sound words, those of our Lord Jesus Christ, and with the doctrine conforming to godliness, he is conceited and understands nothing." This verse applies to false teachers, but I use it to double-check my prayer life. Is my prayer consistent with what Christ taught? Will what I am praying for lead to godliness?

But successful prayer requires more than knowing God's will. It also requires faith, and I have found that my faith works best when I mentally picture what I'm praying for.

PRAYER—PICTURING GOD'S DESIRES

In an earlier chapter I cited two examples of faith: the Roman soldier who exhibited great faith; and the disciples crossing the Sea of Galilee who exhibited little faith. When the storm raged around them they feared losing their lives, even though Jesus had told them they were going to the other side of the lake. The waves crashing over their boat washed away their vision of a safe arrival on the opposite shore. Great faith is knowing, even in the midst of a storm, that we will reach the destination God has given us. Great faith has confidence that it's only a matter of time—a few days, a few years—until we reach God's goals.

Having great faith is impossible without a picture of God's goal in our minds. We need to *see* how we should act with Christ in our life. All of us who know God personally should obey His commands to love Him, value ourselves, and be concerned for the welfare of others. God wants our lives to display the fruit of the Spirit (Galatians 5:22–23).

How will we act when we are loving, full of joy, peaceful, patient, kind, good, faithful, gentle, and self-controlled?

We each need to ask ourselves who we know that exhibits the fruit of the Spirit? Can we say, "That person has life. That's what I want to be like." Though we must not place our expectations in humans, we need examples of men and women totally dedicated to God. The director of a powerful Christian ministry in Europe is a living example to me of how God can shine through us. He exudes life. His facial expressions, warm friendly greetings, and most of all his enthusiasm all convey his total love for Christ. He helps me *see* what Romans 8:29 means when it says that God's desire is for me to become like His Son Jesus Christ.

This also works with specific commands of Scripture. Just as we would use a movie camera to record an event so we could watch it as often as we wanted, our mental cameras can "record" an event that we can play back daily to help us understand how God may answer a prayer. For instance, using God's command to "encourage the fainthearted" (1 Thessalonians 5:14), I picture a scene in much the same way a movie camera would. I may see myself sitting in the living room with a husband and wife who are headed for divorce. They are "fainthearted" and want me to help. I imagine interacting with them, counseling them, and then seeing them emerge from our meeting with renewed hope. If the disciples had done this in Matthew 8, Jesus would have commended them for their great faith. Because they had not "filmed" their arrival on the other shore, they were not able to weather the storm.

God realizes that we need mental pictures in order to grasp His will. When God promised to make Abraham a great nation, He helped Abraham see the promise by showing him the stars of heaven. "So shall your descendants be," God promised (Genesis 15:5). Abraham believed God in spite of one major problem: He had no children. How could he have children as numerous as the stars if his wife couldn't become pregnant? His "storm" lasted for many years. When the fulfillment of that promise was delayed, Sarah tried to help God by having Abraham father a son by her servant Hagar, which proved to be a major disaster. We should beware of running ahead of God's plan and trying to "help" Him with our ideas of how to achieve the goal.

God, in His faithfulness, finally gave them a son when Sarah was ninety years old. But then, unexplainably, God told Abraham to sacrifice his only child. Abraham knew, however, what God had promised so he believed that even if he did kill his son, God could raise him up again. Abraham trusted God because he had pictured the fulfillment of all God had promised him.

This principle of prayer is so powerful that we must be careful how we use it. We might find ourselves receiving something we never really wanted. A classic illustration is the story of the Israelites who cried out for meat in the wilderness after God led them out of Egypt. I can almost hear them chanting, "We want meat! We want meat! We want meat!" It was not God's will for them to have meat; He had already provided manna. But in their stubborn persistence, visualizing the meat they'd had in Egypt, they were relentless. God gave them meat, but with it He sent leanness to their soul. Some translations say they vomited all over the desert.

A common meat-in-the-desert mental picture is lust. When our minds are filled with lustful visions and we imagine the pleasure of lying down with a person other than our spouse, we should be quick to remind ourselves and the Lord that we do not want this fulfilled. Certainly there is pleasure in sin, but only for a short time. Most of us do not realize the devastating effects of extramarital sexual relationships. I once heard a pastor say candidly, "Please, Lord, I never want this vision fulfilled. I do not want to trade the joy of a fulfilling life for the pain of sexual diseases, a calloused soul, a devastated wife, a ruined ministry, loss of self-control, and all the other consequences I don't even know right now. The price is too high."

To protect my prayers I refer again to Psalm 37:4: "Delight yourself in the Lord; and He will give you the desires of your heart." God is number one in my life. No person or thing is of more value to me than knowing Him. Consequently, the most important activity in my life is spending time with Him. As I get to know Him better, I've found that God, through His Spirit in me, gives me specific desires for expressing love to others. There are no limits to what He can do through those who are dedicated to Him.

God could have developed in me a desire to

serve at a mission in Alaska or in an inner-city ministry. He could have called me to continue pastoring or to be a businessman who could support other ministries. The needs around the world are limitless, and God leads His children to love others through an incredible variety of helping ministries. Some serve through a full-time vocation, others through volunteer efforts, and still others give financial and prayer support. Through prayer, we commit to Him the specific desires He gives us. Once I'm convinced God is leading me toward a specific ministry, I begin to pray and picture how He might fulfill the desires He has given me.

Though we're eager to see our desires fulfilled, like Abraham, sometimes we have to wait to see the results of our faith. In the early 1980s, my desire to film my marriage seminar and make it available to families all over the world increased tremendously. I didn't read in Scripture, "Gary Smalley, thou shalt produce a film series." Over a period of several months, however, I asked God about this area and carefully considered if a film would put too much strain on my family or violate any section of Scripture. I also sought the counsel of several Christian leaders. When I finally felt a peaceful confidence that this project would honor God and help His children, I began standing in His prayer line each day.

That's when I started using my imagination, following the direction of Hebrews 11:1. "Now faith is the assurance of things hoped for,"—I hoped to see this film series helping families—"the conviction [or evidence] of things not seen"—I could not hold the film in my hand, but I could see the evidence in my mind. Hundreds of times, while I jogged early in the morning, I saw myself standing under hot lights as a camera crew filmed my marriage seminar. As I mentally lived those film sessions, I also prayed, "Lord, remove the peace if this isn't Your will. I only want to see this happen because I believe it will help Your people. But if it isn't Your will, I'll be glad to step out of line with this request."

Though I never had to step out of line, there were at least two false alarms. One film company wanted me and my board of directors to invest a large sum of money before they filmed. None of us had peace about that. On another occasion, a video company actually filmed my seminar. Apparently they either didn't like it or there were some technical difficulties because they never used it. When these opportunities did not materialize, I got right back into God's line. "Lord," I'd pray, "I really thought this was the answer to my prayer. But apparently it was a false alarm." Then I rethreaded the film in my mind and started running it again day after day, confident that we were going to reach "the other side of the shore." I always believed that before I turned sixty my seminar would be on film. But I always remembered, "Lord, I don't need this film to have fullness in You."

Then in the spring of 1984, the Zondervan Corporation flew one of their representatives to Phoenix. He offered me a contract to do a full, six-part film series. One of the most thrilling aspects of the offer was that without asking me what I had hoped for, he included everything I had already "photographed" in my mind. For instance, Zondervan wanted a follow-up program for the series and dramatic segments in each film, things the other two opportunities did not provide.

Those days were exciting, but they also required a great deal of work. The pressure was even greater than what I experienced with my first two books. I survived only by allowing God "to put His arms around me" and walk through it with me. Though I knew we'd make it to the other shore, there were times when I got so seasick from being tossed around that I could hardly wait for the storm to end.

Let me say that just because I see how God may answer a prayer doesn't mean He is obligated to do it my way. My mental images are only handles to help me grasp God's promises and His will. The actual fulfillment is God's responsibility and He often does it different—and much better—than I imagined. As I seek Him daily, however, making sure I have His desires and believe Him for those desires, I can be assured of one thing—God answers the persistent prayers of His children (see Luke 11:1–6).

Before we leave this section, let me suggest a few cautions. There is a form of mental picturing—some call it "visualization"—that could become an attempt to control our own lives independently from what God would want. As I have mentioned before, God's Word is what guides us at all times. My mental pictures in no way supersede Scripture. They simply do for me what Jesus' parables did for His disciples. They make God's promises as vivid and real as possible.

Today there is a need to biblically balance our understanding of what it means to "picture" something in prayer. On one hand, some leaders encourage us to picture ourselves as fabulously wealthy, promising that if we do we will be. Although the picture may come easily to mind, with all the biblical injunctions against piling up treasures on earth it is difficult to believe that such a goal could be from God.

On the other hand, some condemn as "psychologically based" and ultimately "satanic in origin" any form of picturing things in our minds. If this is taken too seriously it could frighten us away from using word pictures to strengthen our faith, a method that has encouraged believers—even King David— throughout history.

When David sought to capture God's presence during times of deepest trial, the Holy Spirit inspired him to use emotional word pictures. For thousands of years Christians have found comfort in picturing Psalm 23: "The Lord is my shepherd, I shall not want. He makes me lie down in green pastures; He leads me beside quiet waters." Is it wrong to "envision" God as our shepherd? How can a person read these verses and not do exactly that?

A picture paints a thousand words, we often say, and we have many pictures in Scripture to turn to. The Lord is pictured as our rock, our shield, our fortress, our counselor, our rear guard, our gate, and our shepherd, to name only a few. In Revelation 5, Christ Himself is pictured as both a lion and a lamb.

People can abuse mental pictures by either attributing too much power and significance to them or by denying their usefulness altogether. To forbid believers to picture the Lord as their shepherd is tragic and in error. We don't ever want to go beyond what God wills or expresses in His Word, but neither do we want to abandon a method of encouragement He has graciously provided.

Using word pictures or any other "magic formula" will not catapult us to instant spirituality. There is no substitute for a day-by-day, personal walk with Christ. Methods can be practical handles, but they can never solve all our problems. Only through persistent prayer and by spending time in His Word day by day, year by year, can we grow and develop in our love and understanding of God.

PRAYER—ANTICIPATING ANSWERS

Imagine a seven-year-old early Christmas morning. His parents sneak into his room and gently shake him awake so he can join the family in their Christmas celebration. His eyes open, but with a big yawn, he says, "Mom, since I was up so late last night can I sleep for another hour or two? You can open your gifts without me; I'll join you later."

Is this what usually happens? Of course not. The child has anticipated this moment for weeks. He's probably pulling his parents out of bed, impatient to find out what's in the packages under the tree. He has shaken them and examined their shapes, trying to guess what they might contain. He can hardly wait to tear through the wrapping paper.

For me, every day is a little like Christmas. I try

to approach God in prayer like a seven-year-old on Christmas morning. I've prayed some of my prayers for years, yet each day I "get in line" with enthusiastic anticipation, asking, "Is today the day, Lord?" All day I wait to see if one or more prayers might be answered. And when they are, I often receive two packages when I only asked for one. But that only doubles the overflow, for my cup is being filled with Him every day, no matter how many packages I receive—one, two, or none.

Sometimes when I'm reviewing a "Scripture verse film" in my mind, the light bulb burns out or the projector malfunctions. Almost immediately a new film comes into focus showing that God will not be faithful to hear me again. This doubting film is so convincing that if I view it for long, I lose hope. Like when I think, "There's no way God can bring joy this time." I try to shut off the "doubt film" as soon as I recognize it, but sometimes it runs for several minutes no matter what I do.

And sometimes the off-switch fails to work at all. When this happens the only solution is to get up and walk out of the theater. Then later I reenter the theater of faith. And in this case, I'm big on reruns.

What is doubt? Put simply, it is negative faith. Doubt is allowing a film to run through our minds that says "This will never happen to me" or "God can't do this in my life" or "I don't deserve this." Doubt is stepping out of God's line. Doubt is Christ's disciples saying "We'll never make it to the other side." Doubt is the widow giving up and saying she will never receive justice. Imagine if she had gone before the judge for one hundred straight days and then given up hope. She would never have known that had she gone one more day the judge would have granted her request—just to get her out of his hair.

Faith, on the other hand, is the "assurance of things hoped for, the evidence of things not seen." In other words, it is believing that my film imagining the future God desires will eventually become reality. Scripture provides numerous examples. We've already seen how Abraham believed God's promise. Abel, Enoch, and Noah are three more in a long list. Their faith held firm even though God's promises were not fulfilled during their lifetimes. "All these people were still living by faith when they died. They did not receive the things promised; they only saw them [in their minds] and welcomed them from a distance" (Hebrews 11:13 NIV).

PRAYER—USING WORD PICTURES

Word pictures expand the boundaries of our language and thoughts and thereby increase our intimacy with God. They give us a better understanding of God as well as a new way of expressing to Him our thoughts and feelings. God's awesomeness is so far beyond our comprehension that we cannot begin to understand Him unless He expresses Himself in ways we can picture and in settings familiar to our experiences.

David was a master at expressing his relationship with God in word pictures. Look again at some of his visual thoughts: "The Lord is my shepherd. . . . He makes me lie down in green pastures. . . . He leads me beside quiet waters. . . . He prepares a table before me in the presence of my enemies. . . . My cup overflows." Picture with him what he saw when he wrote "You are my hiding place" (Psalm 32:7 NIV), "You are my rock and my fortress" (Psalm 31:3 NIV), and "Your righteousness is like the mighty mountains, your justice like the great deep" (Psalm 36:6 NIV).

Christ Himself helped us "see" who He is by using word pictures. He called Himself the bread of life, the living water, the way, the truth, the vine. And the list goes on and on.

Sometimes I make up my own word pictures: God is my lawyer; He defends me against unjust accusations. He is my architect; He designs a shelter that meets my needs. He is my best friend; I can tell Him anything without fear of rejection. He is my garden; He provides all the nutrients I need. He is my life preserver; He keeps me afloat during life's storms. He is my shelter; He protects me when battles rage. He is my bodyguard; He shields me from attacks.

Often I pray, "Lord, it seems as if all I've done this week is listen to people's burdens. My parched lips and dry, red eyes need Your living water. Let me drink deeply from Your well that never runs dry and splash Your living water over my face. Thank You that You continually satisfy my parched soul. I never cease to be amazed at how fresh You make me feel with so little effort on my part."

PRAYER—LISTENING TO GOD

Prayer is two-way communication. Just as true friendship requires equal participation from each member, so does our relationship with God. We cannot experience the fullness of Christ if we do all the expressing. We must also allow God to express His love, will, and truth to us. (He promised to teach us His knowledge through His Spirit [see Proverbs 1].) We can listen to Him in many ways, but the three I use most often are reading the Word, picturing it, and waiting for His peace.

His Word grabbed my attention one morning as I read James 3. It warned that God will judge teachers more strictly than others. God immediately had my attention. We all stumble in many ways, it said, but those who are able to control what they say are perfect, able to control their whole bodies. James used three word pictures to explain. First, the small bit put into a horse's mouth determines the direction the 2,000-pound animal will go. Second, a small rudder determines the course of a large ship. And third, a small spark can ignite a fire that consumes a whole forest. Our tongues are like the bit, the rudder, and the spark.

Verse eight confused me, however. No one can tame the tongue, it said. I wondered why God would say that those who control their tongues are mature and then say that no one can tame the tongue. I continued reading into chapter 4. In verses 6–10, God revealed the secret of tongue control. James writes that God gives His grace only to the humble—those who recognize their dependence upon Him and allow His power to control them—and that He opposes the proud. God's grace is power in us to control our tongue, but He only gives grace to the humble.

But that was only part of the equation. He continued by saying that if we humble ourselves in His presence, recognizing our complete dependence on Him, He will exalt us. In other words, He will lift us to maturity, which will be reflected in a controlled tongue.

Picturing God's Word in our minds, the second aspect of listening to God, familiarizes us with a verse, a passage, a chapter, even an entire book in the Bible. It is especially helpful when we don't have access to a Bible.

I try to picture God's Word when I'm running or have some idle time. One morning I read the story of how Jesus healed the woman who touched the hem of His garment. Later that day I imagined being at the scene, bringing it to life on my mental screen. I felt and smelled the people pressing around us. I heard the beggars shouting. I saw the lame pushing and shoving, trying to get through. I heard Christ ask who touched Him and I watched the woman tremble as she came forward. I heard Him speak to her: "Daughter, your faith has made you well; go in peace, and be healed of your affliction." Like the disciples, I wondered how Jesus felt one woman's touch among such a crowd. I glimpsed His sensitivity—He cared for someone I and the others had ignored. I saw faith and love firsthand.

Picturing God's Word also helps us apply Scripture. Recently Norma and I have tried to listen to God regarding painful swelling in her knees. Doctors cannot explain the problem. Many Christians have prayed for her, yet she continues to suffer. We can relate to Paul who three times asked God to relieve him of what many believe was a physical problem (2 Corinthians 12:7–10). His problem made him weak, and Norma feels a similar weakness. But Paul also listened. In verse 9 the Lord said, "My grace is sufficient for you, for power is perfected in weakness" and Paul responded, "Most gladly, therefore, I will rather boast about my weaknesses [rather than boast about himself], that the power of Christ may dwell in me. Therefore I am well content with weaknesses, with insults, with distresses, with persecutions, with difficulties, for Christ's sake; for when I am weak, then I am strong." Weakness humbles us and God's grace strengthens the humble.

In his weakness, Paul obtained God's strength—not just for his physical problem, but in numerous circumstances. Because of that truth, Norma and I are praying something like this: "Lord, we've asked You more than three times to heal Norma's knees. You've neither healed them nor given us direction as to how to continue praying. So we'll keep asking for direction. Like Paul we agree that Your grace is sufficient, for power is being perfected within Norma because of her weakness. We are, therefore, grateful for the weakness, knowing that the power of Christ is dwelling in us."

Another way to listen to God is to wait for His

peace. One of the streets on which I jog passes a new development where each lot has a beautiful, panoramic view of Phoenix. A few years ago one lot caught my attention. It was expensive but I figured I could save for it.

Norma and I got in line, praying that God would allow us to purchase the lot so we could build our dream home. Although we never had complete peace about it, I continued to pray. Finally, when we had saved enough money, I checked with the owner and learned that the lot had tripled in price. This forced us to reevaluate God's will in our lives. We determined that His will for us at that time was to use our income in ministry, not in a new home. With that settled, we were free and at peace to stay where we were.

The peace of God should rule in our hearts (Philippians 4:7). One meaning of the Greek word translated *rule* is *to be the umpire.*

Peace, or lack of it, is one way God has of telling us whether we are out or safe, and whether a situation is fair or foul. This does not mean we can never make a decision until we feel some kind of mystical peace. Some people, by their very nature, would never make any decision if they had to wait until they felt peace about it. It means instead that we can be at peace about doing the things God's Word specifically says we should do. For instance, God says we should go to a brother or sister we've offended and ask forgiveness. Therefore we can have peace about doing it even though we feel anything but peaceful on the way over to do it.

As we experience God's peace, hear Him speak to us through Scripture, and see His answers to prayer, we will be motivated to worship and praise Him even more.

PRAYER—PRAISE AND WORSHIP

In the chapter on treasure hunting we discussed one aspect of praise—being grateful for trials—but praise and worship involve many other areas: for instance, singing praise songs, expressing gratitude for His love and generous gifts, and gathering together with fellow Christians for group expressions of love for God. Praise and worship recognize the magnitude of God's great worth. Praising God motivates us to be an expression of His love to others: "This is My commandment, that you love one another, just as I have loved you" (John 15:12).

Prayer undoubtedly encompasses many other areas, areas I am not confident to discuss today, areas that I may not experience until I reach old age. But my desire is for you to experience at least the degree of fullness I have in Christ, to know at least as much as I know of His love, and to experience at least the level of joy and peace He's given me. That will provide us with plenty of reasons to praise and worship our Creator God.

Many have far surpassed me. But for those who feel cheated by life or disillusioned in this relationship with God, I trust this book will be a freshly paved path leading you to a full and lasting relationship with the giver of life, our Lord Jesus Christ.

11

Putting Joy into Practice

YOU MAY WONDER how to implement all we've covered. Unfortunately, although seeing may be believing, reading is not necessarily doing. So I have a few suggestions to make it easier to remember and practice these important truths.

If all we've discussed could instantly become part of our lives, every day we would go to God and allow Him to fill us with His Holy Spirit. We would display His love and joy and peace. Our desires would be His desires. We would get in His line and pray expectantly about the many possibilities of serving others in love.

But it usually doesn't happen overnight. There are too many diversions: getting kids ready for school; hurrying to work; meeting demands from our employer; attending emergency meetings; making a once-in-a-lifetime sale; getting a broken car repaired; visiting a needy friend; resolving a misunderstanding with our spouse—the list is endless. Many of us jump out of bed in the morning, race through the day, and collapse exhausted in bed sixteen or eighteen hours later without giving God a thought, yet wondering all along why our lives are not fulfilled.

One reason we fail to follow through with our well-intentioned commitments is forgetfulness. If we talked about them every day and told others about them, we would be more likely to fulfill them. If everywhere we looked, we saw signs and posters and other tangible reminders, forgetting God's will would be less common.

God understands our forgetful human nature, so throughout the Bible He took great effort to make sure His people didn't forget Him or His commands. In fact, Moses' final instructions to the Israelites before they entered the Promised Land spoke to this issue: "These words, which I am commanding you today, shall be on your heart; and you shall teach them diligently to your sons and shall talk of them when you sit in your house and when you walk by the way and when you lie down and when you rise up. And you shall bind them as a sign on your hand and they shall be as frontals on your forehead. And you shall write them on the doorposts of your house and on your gates" (Deuteronomy 6:6–9).

After several years of going to God daily and praying about how to meet the needs of others, the practice finally became a habit that carried on throughout the day, every day. I had my best time with God when I jogged, but sometimes a business trip or illness or unusually bad weather kept me off the streets, so I sometimes went several days without relating to God. I needed reminders to prompt me to return to Him, no matter what my circumstances. If I couldn't run, I could pray as I showered, drove to the office, sat in an airport or on a plane, took a coffee break, or did chores around the house. Time was available; I just had to concentrate and plan ahead to use it.

Most of us need tangible reminders to help us experience God's fullness. Here are a few ideas:

Buy a special mug to use in the office or your home for coffee breaks. Find one that's painted with a message like "Rejoice in the Lord" or "Love Never Fails" or "Get in God's Line." Each time you use it, take a moment to check the contents of your "internal cup."

Practice these principles with your spouse or a friend. Find someone who will agree to practice with you the ideas in this book for the next seven days or weeks. Check with each other once a day to see how you're progressing. At the end of the seven days you may want to continue your commitment, perhaps reviewing each other's progress once or twice a week instead of daily.

Form a small group that will study these principles. An accountability group will encourage you to go to the Lord for your needs and the needs of others. Report weekly on the progress you've made and reveal your plans for the next week. John Wesley, the founder of the Methodist church, understood this truth. Every day at noon he met with a group of men and reported what he had accomplished the previous twenty-four hours and what he planned to accomplish during the next twenty-four.

List on three-by-five cards the desires God has given you for loving others. Place each card where you will see it at least once a day: the bathroom mirror, by the phone, on the refrigerator, on the dashboard of your car, or on your office desk.

As a family project, make one or more banners or posters to decorate your house. Possible messages might be:

- Are you looking to the Creator or to His creation?

- What does your anger reveal?

- God's will is summed up in these words: Love God, and love your neighbor as yourself.

You might draw a large cup with a spigot over it, and under the drawing print:

- What's filling your cup today?

Memorize a simple prayer for restless nights. Instead of being frustrated when I awake too early in the morning, I thank the Lord that I'm awake and take the time to develop a closer friendship with Him.

Play the "Cup Game" at dinner. Invite family members to tell what God has done in their lives that day. You might include a warning light check. If anyone got angry or had hurt feelings, ask what that revealed. Take time to dream together about each family member's mission and brainstorm about methods that might fulfill the mission. If disappointment or a trial has entered anyone's life, you might want to help that person treasure hunt.

These few ideas will get you started. You might get together with family or friends some evening to come up with more ways to remind each other to walk with God on a daily basis.

I hope by now you have a clear picture of what it means to have a full cup:

- We know our cup is full when negative emotions such as anger, hurt feelings, lust, and worry no longer control our lives.

- We know our cup is full when our negative emotions are replaced by an inner content-ment and love that comes only from God, through Christ.

- We know our cup is full when we recognize that no person or thing in this created world can substitute for the lasting joy of knowing the Creator Himself.

- We know our cup is full when we have learned how to use the painful trials of our lives as rich benefits to us and those around us.

- We know our cup is full and overflowing when we have a clearly defined mission from God to love and serve others.

- We know our cup is full and overflowing when we daily get in God's prayer line, waiting for Him to provide more methods for fulfilling His mission.

My desire is that every believer in Jesus Christ would realize that our joy and peace and fulfillment is not dependent on God's creation. Let's look to the Creator Himself, loving Him with all our heart, soul, mind, and strength. And as He meets our needs, let's look for ways to fulfill His command to love others.

There is no better way to experience lasting fulfillment. And it's open to any and all who *make a decision* to recognize and accept God as the source of JOY THAT LASTS.

Suggested Reading

Happiness Is a Choice, Paul Meier and Frank Minirth, Baker Book House.
Overcoming Hurts and Anger, Dwight L. Carlson, Harvest House.
The Christian Use of Emotional Power, H. Norman Wright, Fleming H. Revell.
The Masks of Melancholy, John White, InterVarsity Press.